One Small Big Step

Shivagam Sranamjiv

F.Lepine Publishing

© Carlos Palmero Zingaro, 2020
ISBN: 978-1-926659-44-2

www.shivagam.com

Translated from Spanish by Ana Paula

Table of Contents

Introduction

Having problems and difficulties is an inevitable part of life, there is absolutely no one who is free from these unpleasant moments. Situations like anxiety, stress, depression, disappointment in life, partner conflicts... are common problems for many people. In addition, we may make the mistake of feeling guilty about being sad and feeling bad or ashamed about having a difficulty and needing help. However, that should not be the case.

You never chose to be depressed or suffer, did you? We don't choose it, sometimes relationships end, sometimes people don't treat you well, sometimes loved ones die, we lose our jobs or we have economic problems. Ultimately, life simply passes and sometimes there is suffering. There is also joy, not everything is negative, but we must accept that pain is real and we experience it.

If you are reading this book it is not by chance, it is not because you have problems, since we all have them. You are here because you are probably tired of them and have decided to do something about it, so you have already taken the first step. Congratulations!

The next step is to understand that behind every problem you have, lies a teaching that only you can discover and understand. And precisely when you find and integrate it, that pain and difficulty will disappear, giving rise first to a state of peace and then to joy. To be more precise, it is not that a teaching emerges as something magical, but that it is a discovery of yourself.

Let's take an example: if I hit my head against the wall, the consequence is that my head will hurt, but since I don't realize what I'm doing, I keep hitting myself while complaining about my headache. As long as I keep doing it, the headache will remain. Well, similar to this example is what happens in the vast majority of your problems: you live and relive them again and again because there is something inside that makes you always behave in the same way, always causing the same results. That is the lesson to be discovered: what must I change within myself, so that this pain and this situation may cease once and for all.

I remember as a child and teenager going from depression to depression, suffering from insomnia since I was 12, and in the mornings, I felt that I had no illusion or motivation in life. Every day I had a panic attack before entering school because of the bullying I was going to receive that day. At age 17, the strong rejection of my sexual orientation and the lack of acceptance, led me back to that state I knew so much: depression. And it was at that moment that something in me woke up and said, "It's impossible that life is just suffering, there must be a way out of here and enjoy."

And that's how I started reading self-help books, taking therapy and courses where I could solve some of my conflicts and complexes. But it wasn't until I learned Emotional Integration that I could really feel that I was getting through the traumas and closing those chapters for good.

Solving all these difficulties not only brought me peace and tranquility, but allowed me to remember that since I was a child, I had had other questions and doubts at an existential level that I had not been able to answer. Why are we here? What am I? What is and how does the Universe work? What is beyond life? Does God exist? These philosophical and spiritual doubts gave me sleepless nights trying to understand them, until when I was 6 years old, I said to myself: "I am too small to understand this and I have no one to explain me, when I grow up, I will solve it." And so it was, feeling so good about myself, about my life, about life in general, that I could then start looking for all these answers, but now in the realm of spirituality, through meditations and even some ascetic practices.

After 6 months of meditating about 2-3 hours a day, suddenly boom! I experienced an explosion of joy, an enormous blessing within me that had nothing to do with the outside, an amount of love and happiness that I had never lived before, in fact, I didn't even know it existed. I had heard something about "joy and inner love" but it sounded more like utopia or hippie philosophy until I experienced it first-hand. To discover that all of that, had really always been within me and that I now had access to those states, was a most beautiful, revealing and transformative experience. I was then 24 years old.

This experience made me realize that at that moment I had already achieved what I was supposed to achieve over a lifetime, what I had dreamed and what everyone is looking for. I had a successful job as an architect, lived in a huge attic with luxury furniture and ocean view, from where I watched the sunrise every day... And then I got the question, "So, now what? What do I have to look forward to for the rest of my life? Keep collecting money and objects?"

What I decided was to go to the other extreme. I gave away all my belongings, got rid of absolutely everything (clothes, books, photos, furniture...) and made a suitcase with 2 pants, 2 T-shirts, a blanket, a coat, a pair of tennis shoes and a pair of shoes; at that time those were all my belongings. I got a one-way plane ticket to Mexico and left behind the whole life I had built. For several months I lived isolated from people, and all I did was meditate 12 to 16 hours a day and sleep. And of course, I achieved a great state of peace, but after 3 months, I felt useless because I wasn't helping anyone or contributing anything to the world.

Feeling good about myself wasn't enough, existing just for me didn't feel right, it felt selfish, I couldn't not share with other people what I learned. This is how I discovered the importance of adapting to today's society and the middle path taught by Buddha. I understood that it was not necessary to be poor and to isolate myself from the world, but we must find the balance in our lives by avoiding extremes and keeping ourselves in the center.

At that moment I decided to go back to society, start building a new life from scratch, get back in touch with people, with my family, and resume the classes, therapies and courses I had stopped. It was more than a desire, a need to help and tell all those people who feel hopeless, without solution: "Hey, your problem has solution, I know because I solved it."

So, these same words are now for you, whether you want to know yourself in depth, or if you want to overcome your conflicts, if you feel hopeless or feel that your problems are very serious and have no solution. Know that it is totally possible to heal, find peace and smile again.

There is not a single problem or emotional trauma that doesn't have a solution if you decide to get up your courage and face it with the appropriate tools. You have to awaken in yourself that same power that I found in me: the knowledge that you will not stop until you overcome your difficulties, accept yourself, discover and love yourself, and start the path to become an Integrated Being, a person who lives in peace, harmony and happiness.

In this book you will find small reflections, easy to read and understand that will help you to open your mind, to consider different perspectives about your difficulties, life and the connection with your essence and even what is beyond yourself.

The book is divided into 4 parts: the first one focuses on the relationship between you and society, your environment, family, work; the second is exclusively about your relationship with you, your complexes, your self-acceptance, your masculine-feminine energy; the third part is about the connection and relationship with your consciousness, with the origin of your individuality, what some call your soul; and finally, the fourth part addresses the universal, that which goes beyond us and is much greater than ourselves, what some call the Divine or Supreme.

Part 1: Sangha

Sangha means "community" in Sanskrit. In Buddhism, it mainly refers to all the people who come together to support and accompany each other on the spiritual path. When we expand its meaning, it includes the relationship with your immediate environment, that is, your family, friends, co-workers and society. This first part is dedicated to our bond and relationship with the *Sangha*.

Shivagam

How to take care of your partner?

Take care of your partner because you love them,
not out of fear of losing them.

When we fall in love and start a relationship, we are very involved, motivated and passionate about the relationship. We give our all to make sure it works and we treat each other like true lovers, showing the best of ourselves.

Then the relationship progresses and it is frequent that people start projects in common that unite them with their partner, such as living together, getting married, having children, getting pets, maybe a business... And there comes a time when all these aspects awaken insecurity and unconsciously, everyone becomes convinced that this is the way to stay together. Time continues to pass and they begin to settle in and neglect each other. They no longer treat each other with the same love of the beginning and even reaches a point where it seems that instead of being a couple, they are enemies, where there are more arguments and claims than displays of love and affection.

They took each other for granted and made the mistake of believing that common projects, responsibilities and commitments are what keeps the couple together, this is not the best way. The greatest and most efficient component of union that can exist is love. This is at the same time the glue that binds them together, as well as gasoline that drives, pushes and makes the relationship evolve.

You should never try to extend and strengthen your relationship by adding more and more commitments or responsibilities, but by adding more and more LOVE, because sooner or later, the first ones will break if there is no love. It's not a question of rejecting commitments, but of letting them happen as a result of love and not of fear of breaking up, or as a control measure or pressure from one towards the other.

In a couple, love is not maintained and generated by itself. This is one of the main mistakes, people do, not taking responsibility for loving and maintaining that love, but hoping that it is maintained as if by magic. It's everyone's responsibility to care for and nurture that love. It's like money; you have to constantly deposit in the joint account so that both can then enjoy it and in case of difficulties have "saved love" to cope with them.

If you have a business and a customer buys you once, you are very happy and grateful. When customers come back for the second or third time you start treating them better and better because they had become loyal customers. The more they come back to your store, the better you treat them, the more benefits you offer and the better you make them feel. Every time they come back; you give them more reasons to return for the next day. It would never occur to you to take them for granted, treat them badly or cheat on them because you know that they could buy at any other store and you would lose a good customer.

Well, your partner is your best customer. A partner is a totally free person who does NOT have the obligation to buy in your "store", doesn't have a long-term contract with you. Partners don't have to continue the relationship, they don't have to love you, it's not their obligation, but a choice. Your partner is a totally free person who doesn't belong to you.

How much do you take for granted that "your partner has to love you", "to be with you", to take care of you and support you? How much have you taken your partner for granted?

And how many motives or reasons do you give your partner to choose you as that customer to the store?

For a relationship to work in the long term, it is essential that both get out of that "taking for granted" mood, of that settling in the relationship, and realize that they must give their partner countless reasons so that, among all the options there are, they keep choosing each other every day.

May this choice be for love and benefits, not for pressure and control, not for mutual responsibilities, not through imposing fear, but through nurturing the relationship, caring for and loving each other.

If when a partner gets home, the first thing they receive are complaints, claims and yelling… would you treat a good customer that way? Do you think that will bring them closer or further away from you? You are creating a battlefield instead of a comfortable home where both can be happy. Your partner (and you) don't have the obligation to return home each day, it must be a voluntary choice. Therefore, each day that both of you come back, should be considered with gratitude because you are both free not to do it. This keeps you constantly grounded and prevents you from falling into that over certainty so that you always remain caring for each other and nurturing the relationship through love. This way you will hold the relationship from love and not from control.

Once you are clear that you must take care of each other, the question is how? How to make the person you love feel cared for?

Consider that you have your way of being, your likes and dislikes. You know how you want to be cared for and pampered, that is why you think everyone likes and needs the same as you, but it is not like that. Everybody has their singularity and different needs and tastes. Therefore, what makes you happy may be that your partner or family is not interested or doesn´t generate the same emotion of joy or excitement that you.

For example, remember when you went to buy a gift for a friend who has tastes contrary to you and you found a shirt that you knew she was going to love, but you didn´t like. Then you said: "I can't give something I don't like; I have to be honest with myself." And you finally bought a shirt that you loved, but your friend didn't. Did you really take good care of your friend? The shirt was not for you. How do you feel when someone gives you something you don't like?

Breathe.

Looking after your partner or loved ones is based on taking care of them the way THEY need, not the way you want to do it. So, you have to sacrifice your preferences for a short period of time. You must understand that this moment is to make the other person happy not you, but you can enjoy it through seeing happy the one you love. Then another time it will be the other way around.

Another example is when you wanted to invite your partner to a romantic dinner and what you did was going to YOUR favorite restaurant. Isn't this selfish? If the perfect evening for your partner is to have a hamburger on the couch with a beer watching TV with you, would you do it to make your partner feel pampered? Or would you think, "This is boring, it's not romantic, I don't like it, so I don't want to do it"? If you want to pamper your partner, you must agree to do what the other one will enjoy.

Remember when your partner gave you a surprise exactly as you wanted it, when you received exactly what you wanted, or your partner took you to that place that you like so much; at that moment your heart exploded with love and happiness. At that moment, you had no eyes for anyone else and the relationship strengthen. That feeling is what you have to create for your partner. Then your partner will feel terribly pleased with you. With this, you will have set the wheel in motion in the relationship and now your partner will also want, naturally, to take care of you.

One of the problems that keeps us from taking care of each other is that everyone always wants to receive before giving, but it must be the other way around, first giving and then receiving. Sometimes it happens that you are waiting for your partner to do something for you and as he or she doesn't, you do nothing either and you think "if he / she does nothing, neither do I". This is pride. For a relationship to stay alive there has to be movement and someone has to start giving to make the wheel turn. Don't expect the other to initiate the movement, initiate it yourself. Dare to be the one to break that pride and start giving.

Look at it from this perspective: when someone gives you a gift for no reason, immediately afterwards you feel that you are in debt and that now you owe them something. The same happens in relationships: take care of your partner first and this will make your partner feel the desire and need to take care of you. So, both of you will be making the relationship flow and there will be no monotony. You will be taking care of love, together.

On the other hand, just as you have taken care of your partner in your own way up to now, understand that your partner has been doing the same. Probably when you complain about your partner not careening for you, it is not like that, the problem is that your partner doesn't do it your way, so you don't feel cared for. Don't blame it on your partner, have compassion and forgiveness because you have done exactly the same. The solution is to sit down and talk honestly and calmly. First ask your partner: "Honey, how do you need me to pamper and take care of you?" and try to understand and remember what they say. Do not take it as a reproach, but rather that you are finally getting to know each other from that perspective. Then with total clarity and no hints you say "Honey, when you want to pamper me, this is what I like" and you give your partner your list. Then you will know each other's needs and how to satisfy each other.

Finally, learn to distinguish when you want to make another person feel good from when you want to feel good. When you want to pamper the other, do it their way and when you want to pamper yourself, say it honestly, then it's time to do it your way. It's not selfish to ask to be taken care of as you need, it is selfish if you only want others to take care of you and you don't want to do the same for them.

An exercise that you can practice in the next few days, is to make the effort and take care of your partner or loved one in its 100% form. Focus on making the other person feel happy and pleased in their own way. When you do, observe the expression of happiness and love in that person, then you will catch that joy and your satisfaction on that occasion will be watching the person you love happy, knowing that you are the cause of that joy. After doing it for 2 or 3 days, watch how the dynamics of the relationship change, now there is love in motion again.

The more you take care of each other in the relationship, the more satisfied will both be, the more happiness and love you will feel and the more desire to continue together you will have.

Take care of your partner from love and not from control.

Open yourself to life

*To force everything to be exactly like you
want it without ever sacrificing yourself, is control.*

Competitiveness is born from the idea of limitation of resources, of superiority. Whenever you consider that there is not enough for everyone, you start to compete to ensure your survival. It is something innate in us as human beings.

Metaphorically, you look at a field and you see that there is only one orange tree with 3 oranges and there are 10 people who want those oranges, so you feel like you have to fight and compete for them. This happens because you are wearing "donkey blinkers" that only allow you to see a portion of the field, you can only see what is right in front of you, but you can't see the sides. The reality is that, if you took off those blinkers, you would discover that you are in the middle of an infinite field of oranges, apples, pears, etc., and that you just have to walk peacefully without fighting anyone, towards any of those trees full of fruits, and eat everything you want.

What are these donkey blinkers made of?

Control, among other things. You live wanting to control everything. You don't want "a" job, but it has to be the job that You want, in the place that You want and earning what You want. You don't accept to live in "any" comfortable place, but you want to live where you want to live. You don't accept your partner as he or she is, but you want them to be as you want them to be. And so on with every aspect of your life, which keeps you in a constant state of dissatisfaction and frustration.

Forcing everything to be exactly how you want it to be, without ever sacrificing anything, is control. And because you don't have the house, partner, job or money you want, you are convinced that it's because there is not enough and you start to compete with others who are also wearing donkey blinkers.

Sometimes you can choose and do things to your liking and preferences, but there will be times when you must agree to make certain sacrifices. If you want to work on what you like, you have every right to do so, you must strive to make it happen, but you may have to sacrifice how or where it will happen.

Decide what you want in life, take off your blinkers, take control, broaden your look and contemplate the entire field, then you will discover which areas of the field are infertile and should be avoided, and which are fertile to cultivate them successfully.

Competing with other people or companies is fighting against them for your own benefit and every fight becomes a cause of suffering always. In a fight or war, there are never winners, everyone suffers. While you are in the competition, you are nervous and stressed about winning. Then if you lose, you suffer for losing and if you win, your pride increases and in the next competition you will have more stress and anguish because you have to maintain the previous victory, and at some point you will lose and suffer the accumulation of everything.

Sometimes you compete to prove your superiority or worth to yourself and others. Wanting to show how good you are, is born from an inner emptiness that you intend to fill by being better than others. That void is the right to life, you want to convince yourself that you have the right to that job, to that partner, to that house, to that promotion, to success. But it doesn't matter how hard you try to show your worth because it always seems not enough for your parents, your boss or your partner, and you often don't get the validation that you are looking for from them. You cannot live your life based on others, or pressure your environment to recognize you. You must take your power and your place in life; nobody is going to give it to you because nobody has it. Your place in life is either taken by you or it's simply empty.

There is no human being with more value or importance than another. Nobody has more right to life than you and you have no more right to life than anyone else. We all come from the same origin and our biological process is exactly the same, so we are all the same.

Your studies, preparation, culture, money, actions, etc., don't make you better than others. This don't make you deserve something more than others; it just makes you very efficient or competent in a certain field, that's all. Of course, you are entitled to the experiences you want, but others are also entitled to their own experiences.

For example, if we wanted to test the performance and efficiency of two phones from different brands and put them side by side to work to the fullest, the phones will not be looking to sabotage, compare or discredit each other. Each phone is simply giving as much as it can within its efficiency and competence. That should be your attitude in your work and in life: don't compete against anyone, instead show 100% of your efficiency and competencies.

When the Sun rises in the morning, it doesn't analyze each human being to see how much light and heat it is going to give each one. The Sun just shines. Some go out to take and receive that sunlight and others hide under an umbrella complaining that there is not enough sunlight and refusing to go out of the shade, but the Sun is not the one that makes the distinction.

Metaphorically, this Sun is life's opportunities. Life doesn't distinguish between anyone. Life creates constant and infinite opportunities exactly the same for everyone and some take advantage of them, and others hide on the shadow and in their blinkers. You have to get out of the shadow, agree to make some sacrifices, make an effort, look up and the Sun and life will be shining for you as well as for others.

An exercise to identify your "umbrellas" is to think about your goals, desires and dreams, and with complete honesty towards yourself, pay attention to whether you feel that you deserve and have the right to achieve it and have it. You will see that there is a part of you that doubts and denies the possibility, you will see all the thoughts and ideas of self-sabotage that are in you. All this is the "umbrella" that keeps you away from your goals, believing that you have to fight to get them, and even go against others.

Now that you have identified them, you have two responsibilities: the first is to work on yourself to consciously feel these resistances; study, analyze and understand them in order to eliminate them. The second is to develop confidence and security in yourself and in your right to life. Meditate, repeat and contemplate "I have the right to life, I have the right to be happy" and by doing so, make sure not to tell anyone, it is not the others who need to know this, it's you, who must accept and understand this.

The Yelling

A yell is just heavy metal music at a very high volume.

Occasionally you were talking with your partner about the organization of the family economy, you didn't agree on something and the conversation became an argument until reaching the "don't yell at me", "I AM NOT YELLING AT YOU", "YES YOU ARE YELLING AT ME", "THE ONE THAT IS YELLING IS YOU ". And at that moment, you even forgot what you were talking about and everything focused on the shouting and the offenses.

On another occasion, you got angry with your boss because he scolded you, you didn't yell at him because the fear of losing your job was greater than the anger, but that desire stayed inside of you. Hours later when you got home you exploded and yelled at your partner or children for any nonsense, and in reality, what you did was unload the frustration of your job on them, which had nothing to do with the home issue.

When someone yells at you, you get offended and react. Sometimes it even activates your fear and blocks you without knowing what to say or how to act, and other times it's your pride that speaks and says "Who do you think you are to yell at me?" The first step to handling these situations is to realize that, as much as you want, you can't control how others express themselves or speak. You live in society, where each person is different, you can't expect everyone to be kind, polite and speak to you the way you want, because it's not going to happen. It's normal that you don't like being yelled at, but you have no control or power over anyone to change them. However, what you can do is learn to manage your reaction so that when something like this happens, you know how not to take it personally and stay at peace.

To help you understand, remember the last time you yelled at someone. Contemplate: Did you choose to get angry and yell? Was it a conscious decision?

And the answer is No. Every time you get angry and yell, it´s not a choice that you make, but something within you reacts, takes over and you explode without being able to control yourself. Remember how many times in your mind you are saying "I'm not going to yell; I'm not going to yell" and "Ahhhhh ..." the yelling happened. No matter how hard you tried, you couldn't hold back because it´s not a choice, but an automatic reaction to your internal frustrations and disappointments. In the end, you couldn't not yell.

Well, you must understand that the same happens to others, they don´t choose to shout either, it is not a choice and even if they want to control themselves, they still cannot.
The next step is to pay attention to how you feel when you yell at someone. There is probably frustration, hatred, anger or rage. Therefore, we can say that when you yell it´s because you are having a hard time, right? It is precisely the pressure of pain that, being so intense, makes you unable to control and explode. So now you know what others feel when they yell. Like you, they don't choose it either, they are being victims of anger and pain. They yell at you because they are suffering at that moment.

From this point of view, how compassionate it is to stick your finger in someone else's wound? Yelling back is counterattacking someone who is suffering. When you yell at someone and they yell even louder, it is because their wound is open and you are throwing stones at them.

Breathe.

It is normal for a part of you to think "they are yelling at me and above all I must have compassion for them?" This is because you are still taking it personally. You are still considering that they "yell at you", so we need to continue in the study of yelling.

In these events it is your pride that reacts and wants to defend itself, but yelling back has never ended the problem, in fact it always makes it worse, because you can even say things and insults that you will regret later. Yelling from this point of view, is trying to impose on each other, but if you are not right, yelling more isn't going to give it to you, and if you are right, not yelling won't take it away.

If you contemplate that no one chooses to yell and that it's a reaction to internal emotional pain, then you can understand that no one ever yells at you as such; they yell because they suffer and you happen to be in front. Even if in the choice of words or forms it looks like they are yelling at you for something you did or said, it's still their pain that makes them yell. You must learn not to take it personally when it happens and remember these lessons.

When you understand this deeply, you can change your perception and discover that they are not even yelling, but are SPEAKING VERY VERY LOUD because they feel bad and you happen to be in front at that moment.

The next time yelling happens, take a deep breath and remember "they are not yelling at ME, they are just yelling because they are in pain and they are not even yelling, they are just expressing themselves very, very loud and I am just in front". Don't dramatize or take it personal. Find out what reacts in you when it happens, observe your pride and make the decision not to take it personally, even if you find it hard, also think about the person who is yelling and put yourself in their shoes to understand their suffering.

The best thing at that moment, if you can't control yourselves, is to accept that you are upset and responsibly choose to continue the conversation when you have calmed down a bit.

Then be responsible and if possible, tell the other when they are calm, how you feel when they yell. Invite them to observe their disappointment and take charge of it, to understand that yelling does not give or take away reason and that speaking calmly always gives better results. When we get upset like this we don't think clearly and we are not objective. If they don't change, take some distance if the situation allows it, out of compassion for you and so that the other person understands that this is not the way to relate each other in a respectful and compassionate way. If you cannot communicate your feelings because the other person is closed-minded or it is a specific case, and you cannot take distance yourself either, then at least it won't bother you that they "speak out".

Finally, when you are the one who yells, it´s normal that at first you don't remember these teachings until after you have yelled. Little by little you will notice more quickly, until a point comes when you will remember this during your yelling. At the very moment you realize you are going to explode, if you can, take a deep breath from your abdomen, close your eyes for 2 seconds during this breathing and repeat "I am aware that I am aware, I am not angry but disappointed, I give up" and breathe deeply again. This "I surrender" mood, is a way of telling your brain that you are not going to start a fight, it has nothing to do with the person in front of you, nor with the problem itself. Giving up here is accepting that you are suffering. By doing so and repeating this phrase a couple of times, your desire to explode and yell will most likely subside. Then you must do your self-therapy work to finish solving your pain.

A yell is just heavy metal music at a very high volume and an insult is just a word to which you give the intention and importance you want. Stop giving the power of your mood to others or their words.

Projection vs. Responsibility

You are responsible for everything and guilty of nothing.

If there is a fire near you, you naturally run away from it to avoid burning. This is an innate reflex to avoid pain and ensure survival. We are programmed to run away from pain. But just as in the case of fire or external danger, we also do this within ourselves with our discomfort, because it is something innate.

Every time you feel bad, you try to run away from suffering like from fire, by going shopping, going to the movies or drinking alcohol. Other times, you try to run away by blaming and projecting your pain on others and on life. And after several attempts you realize that it doesn't work because your nightmares haunt you down. It's not that your pain follows you, it's that suffering is inside of you and it doesn't matter where you run or who you want to blame, it follows you because it is in you.

All these unhealed wounds and scars create within you what we call "potentials for suffering." These potentials (sadness, loneliness, anger, disappointment, etc.) are not always active, but combined with all the other positive potentials (peace, harmony, joy, awareness, etc.) and flow, moving like a lava lamp. When an anger potential heats up, it wakes up, rises to your perception and you get angry. If you don't dissolve that potential, after a certain time it cools down and "goes to the bottom", and lays there asleep until it is awakened again causing you a new anger.

On the other hand, when a potential for joy heats up, it is awakened, it rises and now you feel joyous and that joy stays until it cools down or until a potential of anger heats up and pushes the joy to the bottom. Even on some occasions, different potentials blend into your perception and that's when you don't even know how you feel. You have a feeling of sadness, but at the same time you feel happy, it makes no sense feeling sad and happy at the same time. This is why; each potential is different and it may happen that both are awake at the same time.

The solution is not to cool down the suffering potentials, as they will wake up again at some point. The ultimate solution is to eliminate them from within by observing them and staying aware of them until they disappear.

What heats up your potentials?
Remember every time you have eaten a special holiday dish, like a dessert or roast. Have you noticed that after the first bite, the next thing everyone does is compare it to the last time and the last place you had it? It's automatic, everyone says which one is tastier and which is the best place where that dish is prepared. This happens because all the similar experiences that you have lived are interconnected and when you experience one of these situations again, the entire chain of those experiences is activated in your subconscious. Therefore, when you eat that special dish, you automatically awaken your chain of those special dishes in full. That is why if one day you were poisoned by eating certain food, you don't want to eat that again because just the sight of it awakens the chain of indigestion from the last time.

Suppose now you have a complex because you are fat, because you are not good enough for your parents, because of your sexual preference or of any other issue. That complex is a latent experience within you and the moment someone names it, the memory of each time you have felt that way is automatically awakened -just as it happened with food- and you feel offended without choosing it.

Because you are now offended, the next thing you do is project that discomfort onto another person, the trigger. You must realize and understand that what bothered you was not what that person told you, what hurts are the potentials within you that woke up and exploded. And because what awakened that chain was the person in front of you, you project and blame him or her for your discomfort, but the reality is that the discomfort was already latent inside of you. The complex, which is what makes you suffer, is already inside of you.

That projection gets you stuck in "How dare you say or do this to me?" and in showing you and others that this is a bad person for what he or she did. Let's suppose for a moment that the person who offended you is actually a bad person and should never have done it, it's a fact. Realize who is still suffering? You. Blaming others for your discomfort doesn't relieve you, because discomfort is inside you and you are the only one who can heal it. Blaming yourself for your discomfort is also not good, because it puts pressure on you and takes you to victimhood. The solution is responsibility. You are responsible for everything you live and feel, and guilty of nothing.

This doesn't mean that what they said or did to you was ok, it means that regardless of what happened, you are the only responsible for healing your pain; no one can do it for you. You will only find the solution when you stop projecting on others and decide to take responsibility for it.

When you have an argument and you feel insulted or offended, try to identify which chain of potentials has awakened, so that you can take responsibility and eliminate those potentials. Remember that if something affected you, it affected you, and you can't help it, but you can heal it.

Finally, responsibility also implies that, if someone is constantly attacking you, bullying you or doesn't treat you kindly, you must say how you feel and if that person does nothing about it, then ponder why do you want such a person in your life? Just walk away from that person for your own sake. Your well-being and happiness are your responsibility.

A correct conversation

No one should suffer for you to have fun.

Speaking is the main form of communication and interaction that we have in society, whether speaking in person or through technology, such as social networks and mobile phones. Therefore, you must observe what your attitude is when speaking and how you affect your environment with your conversations.

In Buddhism there is the Noble Eightfold Path, which are 8 basic steps for good behavior with ourselves and with others. In this path, the third step is known as "Right Speech." On many occasions it has been explained as not lying, however, that is only a part. If we were to sum it up in one sentence, a right speech or correct conversation is "that way of communicating in which, through compassion, you always avoid causing suffering to everyone."

For example, imagine you have a friend who never takes care of herself and puts on the first thing she finds. Then one day she comes home dressed in pink floral shirt and orange striped trousers, with an exaggeratedly face made up, so when you see her you think "What a disaster!" If you mock or tell her that she looks terrible, because you have to always be honest, you just wrecked your friend's attempt to take care of herself and maybe decide to put her old clothes back on and never try again. On the other hand, if you say "How nice you look!", you are lying and, on the street, people will laugh at her. A proper conversation here would be to tell her how much you appreciate that she's decided to take care of herself and change her look, since as a friend it's true, and then invite her to go shopping so you can recommend what's good for her and what's not. This way you are not lying, but you are not destroying her intent either; your friend will now feel supported, respected and you will be helping her.

Another kind of harmful conversation is gossip, criticism and making fun or laughing at others: talking for the sake of talking; criticizing without most of the time, not even knowing if what they are saying is true or not; using humor or jokes based on ridiculing or offending someone. All these conversations produce discomfort, misunderstanding and suffering to everyone involved. Think how many misunderstandings and how many friendships have been broken because of this.

It is not fair that, for you to have fun, someone has to suffer. There are many ways to laugh, to enjoy life and friendship, many topics to talk about without having to hurt anyone. Just like you don't like being criticized, gossiped, or laughed at, nobody likes it. Just don't do it!

When you feel the need to tell something that you don't know if it's true or if it's going to be useful to someone, don't do it. When you feel like gossiping, criticizing someone or lying, take a deep breath and ask yourself: What in me is pushing me to say it? Find the emotion that is pressing you. It's that discomfort that convinces you to say it and then repent. That emotion is often a void or an emotion of loneliness and abandonment. Breathe, feel the discomfort and then find a way to fill that gap through meditation, for example. A good meditation for self-filling is to breathe and remain conscious of your breathing. Feel the air coming in and out of your lungs. You can do it for a few minutes a day or when something inside you wants to say something that isn't appropriate.

To have a correct conversation avoid lies, gossip, criticism and humor based on ridiculing others. Even if you know some facts about someone, but you realize that they will not be useful, nor will they help anyone, don't say it.

On the other hand, when you know something that is true and can be beneficial for others, don't rush to tell it also, wait for the best time and the best way to do it. Sometimes this conversation may hurt someone, but if you are compassionate and conscious, this harm will prevent a bigger damage.

Now, when you communicate with others, it may happen that you try to explain something to someone and you are super clear, for you it's obvious, but the other person doesn't understand or misunderstand you. You try again and it seems to make the misunderstanding worse and that the other person only hears one sentence and not all the content.

This happens because you have a way of seeing life, your own way of thinking, expressing yourself and doing things. You have been doing this for a long time and this makes part of you convinced that this is the best way possible, since, if you knew of a better one, you would change it. The same thing happens to every person you interact with. Everyone is convinced that "their" way is the ideal and perfect one, but each of these ways are different from the others. This is what causes not to understand each other and even to be offended, because they don't agree in the way and form of each other.

In the same way, every time someone talks to you, you don't listen to their words, but you pass them through your personal filter and interpret them in your own way. But often there are mistakes and misunderstandings in interpretations. Think on how many times you give an intonation and an intention to a message or comment you read on Facebook, Twitter or WhatsApp, getting upset for how they say it to you. Then you answer accordingly and now the other person does exactly the same thing, interpret it and you end up angry, arguing over what you both supposedly said, when in reality it was a simple and silly misunderstanding due to the difference in styles.

The problem with communication is that you don't speak so that the other understands, but to say what you want to say. You are more concerned with saying what you want than with the other person understanding. It's like talking to a Russian in Spanish and pretending they understand; such communication is impossible and everyone gets frustrated. It seems the same, however they are totally different things. When you only want to say what you want, you don't consider the other's way of speaking, your choice of words, their way of being, etc., you just say it. Whereas when you take others into account, now you use their words, metaphors, expressions... then they understand perfectly.

A good communicator is someone who is able to adapt and speak as others need and not as he or she wants to say things. Then the message is transmitted and understood.

It's not just putting yourself in each other's shoes, but now talking from those shoes. Adapt to others. To do this, let go the pride of your way of doing and saying things, accept that other people have their ways and they also work well for them. This doesn't mean you will stop being yourself, as it's a momentary adaptation to a better relationship and understanding, but you will remain as you are.

Some good tips for a correct conversation are:
• When you talk to someone, listen to the words they use and try to use them when you speak.
• Try to understand what they want to tell you without adding any personal interpretation and ask what you don't understand.
• When they tell you something that bothers you, before getting offended, ask them what they mean and what is the intention of their words, you will save yourself a lot of anger.
• Don't be afraid to communicate, to sit down and talk as much as necessary, from a calm and open-minded attitude.
• If you realize that you have made a mistake, ask for forgiveness; that is humility and will help the other person feel better.
• First listen to others, then ask to be heard.

How to forgive?

To forgive is not to agree with anyone,
It is to realize that if you don't forgive, you suffer.

Think of someone with whom you are angry at (your ex, a friend, your mother ...), now think for how long you have been angry... weeks, months, maybe years. Probably they have moved on and may not even remember you or even your name and yet you are still upset today, and you don't even want to talk about it because you feel a knot in your stomach. How long do you want to go on with the suffering?

The problem is that you think if you forgive you are agreeing with them and that then you've lost. You think forgiving justifies what they did to you, but it doesn't. When conflict happens, one thing is the event itself and another thing is the emotion or pain that the event caused. Justice must take care of the event; Forgiveness releases the suffering caused.

To forgive means to understand that all this time it has been you who has been and continues to suffer. It doesn't matter if what the other person did was right or wrong, whether it was fair or not, as long as you don't forgive, it still affects you.

One of the hardest experiences some people have had is physical abuse or rape. These events, due to the intensity of pain, become the most traumatic and difficult events to forgive because forgiveness is confused with justifying what happened. In order to overcome these experiences, it is necessary to expand and make a change of perception to de-dramatize the event.

Surely at some point in your life you have hit your shin with the corner of a table or kicked a chair with your bare foot. Can you remember that moment? The pain was very intense, it even left you a bruise that lasted for weeks, but you didn't get angry at the chair or the table, you didn't stay offended at the furniture because you know it was just an accident and later on you didn't even remember what happened. Well, if someone has ever physically beaten you, you can remain traumatized by the situation and blaming the aggressor for years, limiting your life, your relationships and even your sexuality ... Or you can make a big effort to change your perception and realize that you were not hit, you just "stumbled" that person's hand or fist.

Breathe, I know it's hard, but consider it for a moment. It may even be that the blow with the chair or some fall was even more painful than the blow received. When something like this happens, you get stuck in the injustice and blaming the aggressor, but the real pain is inside of you. What happened was not fair, you should get away from that person and report to the authorities to prevent it from happening again to you or someone else. But realize that even if that person is arrested and taken to prison, your pain and trauma will not go away, because one thing is justice and another is forgiveness.

That's why, if you really want to overcome it, you must stop blaming others or seeking revenge because that is looking on the outside. That's not where the pain is. Change your perception, you were not hit, you tripped and you hit someone's hand. It wasn't your fault either, it just happened. Don't blame the aggressor, don't blame yourself, just observe the pain of the situation and choose to forgive.

This need to project blame and not wanting to forgive because it is very painful, is your pride. When someone offends or hurts you, the situation itself lasts for a while, then it's you who lengthens and extends the pain and trauma. There is nothing unforgivable. When you say "what they did to me is unforgivable" you are choosing to remain in drama and suffering.

When you have this feeling, take the first step and change the "there can be no forgiveness" to "I can't forgive this" and remain aware, paying attention for a few minutes to the fact that it's very hard and difficult for you to forgive. It's not impossible, it's just that you can't do it right now. But if you consider it this way, then you will realize how much you have suffered for not forgiving. This will take you to the second step: it's not that you can't forgive, it's that you don't want to forgive. This is the real problem, there is a part of you that is not willing to forgive and let go of the problem, this is your pride.

An offense or blow hurts a couple of days, maybe weeks, but your hurt pride can last for years and years. To forgive, is to understand that nobody has the key to living a perfect life, and when we interact with other people, we sometimes hurt ourselves because in many ways we are incompetent and we don´t know how to act or how to behave. We are all learning to live and we all do the best we can. When you choose to forgive, you choose to stop suffering and also help the other to learn from their mistakes. This way both can evolve and improve.

Forgiving doesn´t mean enduring the repetitive unconsciousness of others either. If someone constantly offends you or annoys you, you must forgive them so that you don´t suffer, but then you must be responsible to yourself and make them understand that they are hurting you. If they don't change their attitude, forgive them and step back. Walk away, not out of resentment or anger, but out of respect and compassion for yourself. Perhaps this way they will finally realize that this attitude makes them lose those they love.

Forgiveness is a very emotional virtue as it reminds you that sometimes you made mistakes and someone suffered for it. You didn't do it on purpose, but it happened. Likewise, it happens with others, in most cases, they didn´t do it on purpose. When you forgive, if there is love left, it now flows again and if there is none left, a state of peace, understanding and respect simply remains.

It´s time now to let go of your pride and your fear and agree to forgive. It´s time for you to agree to free yourself from that burden that has been with you for too long.

Do this exercise: Take a deep breath, accept that this problem is affecting you, don´t fight it anymore. Accept that you are tired, that you want to solve it and from this will to heal and feel good, think of that person with whom you are upset or hurt and repeat in your mind the word *Anuja* (it is pronounced "anuya" and it means "forgiveness" in Sanskrit) and in the meantime, pay attention to your breathing and occasionally take a deep breath. Do it until all the pain and offense of that problem is gone, then you have freed yourself from that burden.

I forgive
It doesn't matter if I understand it or not.
I forgive
It doesn't matter if I agree or not.
I forgive
It doesn't matter if it was good or not.
I forgive
It doesn't matter if I liked it or not.
I forgive
It doesn't matter if I was wrong or if it was you.
I forgive
Because I understand that we all make mistakes.
I forgive
Because it is the key to the liberation of my suffering and yours.
I forgive
Because forgiveness closes the gates of my own hell and opens the gates of heaven.

I forgive, and you?
FORGIVE

The Police

I love the police.

About 800 years ago family members could not sleep at the same time because someone could break into the house to steal, rape or kill them, so one of them kept watch all night. Usually the father and the firstborn took turns. Today we have come a long way and when night falls, you close the door of your house and everyone sleeps peacefully, completely ignoring danger.

At that time, if anything happened to you, you had no one to ask for help, you were alone in the face of danger and you were the only one willing to defend your family. Today you dial a phone number and the police come to your aid. Cops put their lives at risk every day so that we can ignore the dangers and get on with our lives. They face what we don't want to face.

The police don't want to bother you, they are not against you. They take care of everyone and if you commit any fault or crime, you must be responsible and accept the consequences. When they act to protect you and for your benefit you love them, but when you do something wrong and they protect others from you, now you hate them. That's not being fair, it's childish.

Before complaining about the police, you should ask yourself how many bad experiences you've had directly with them. If you've had any problems, see how most of the time it was because you got a ticket when you ran a traffic light or committed an infraction. Were you responsible for it? In that case, the police were not going against you but teaching you what not to do. That is their job and your responsibility is to pay the fine, not try to evade it or persuade them in any legal or illegal way not to give it to you. If you do that, now you are the corrupt one.

On many other occasions your complaint is based on what happened to a friend's friend. Do you remember playing Chinese whispers? In that game the information was transformed as it passed from mouth to mouth, just as when that third person told you something that a friend of a friend lived. What is more real, what you have lived for yourself or what a friend of a friend says? You must be objective and based on first-person experiences. If you've had a bad experience where they did something inappropriate, don't generalize to everyone and then look for a way to sue for justice.

Does this mean that the current police are perfect? No, it's not, it can get a lot better, but it's not true to say that they don't do anything right or that they are all corrupt or bad and just want to annoy people.

It is common to get defensive when a police officer approaches, or to even to insult them. Have you ever stopped to think how a lot of people hate them? Criminals hate them. Those who don't commit crimes also hate them because they represent authority and are afraid of getting scolded for, so everyone hates them. Surely you have been with someone who doesn't like you and you know how uncomfortable it is. Can you imagine the stress a police officer endures, always receiving insults from everyone, no one valuing their work and still risking their lives for those who insult them?

You must change your perception and attitude. Instead of projecting hate, support them, consider them with compassion and understanding. You must accept the authority they represent, not as superiority but as those who maintain balance and protect us. When you come across them on the road, yield, whether or not you understand why they have the siren on or where they're going. It's none of your business and most likely they're going to help someone in need. That someone could one day be you or your family and you will want help to arrive as quickly as possible.

If they stop you, do not get defensive, do not counterattack, just answer their questions, their job is to investigate. They don't know you so it's normal for them to doubt you, don't take it personally. If you have done nothing wrong, then you have nothing to hide, tell the truth and everything will be fine. Collaborate with them.

Respect the police and even more important, teach the children and teenagers the importance of their role in society so that they too can grow with that respect for authority. Having a better police force is a team effort, they must improve and we must value them, appreciate their presence and respect their instructions.

If you change your attitude towards them, when you see them you will feel protected, sheltered and blessed because someone who doesn't know you, cares about you and the safety of your loved ones. So, every time you hear a siren, instead of being bothered by the noise, feel calm because you know they are there, whether you need them or not.

I love the police.

Special days on the calendar

Any day is a good day to love, enjoy, be happy and take care of your loved ones.

The calendar is full of special days such as Valentine's Day, Christmas Eve, New Year's Eve, anniversaries, birthdays, etc., they are days for celebration. However, on many occasions these turn into arguments and problems. Every time you feel bad for not being able to celebrate as you expected, you are allowing that day to have power over you.

For example, Valentine's Day, is the day of "Love and Friendship" ... and broken hearts. Some celebrate the day with gifts and special dinners with their partners, others argue because one of them forgot the day, others because one of them has to work and many others suffer because they do not have a partner. How can one day affect you so much?

What makes February 14, December 24 or your birthday a special day?

It dawns at the same time, it gets dark at the same time, the planet rotates the same as other days. Your work routine will probably be the same and your dog or cat behaves exactly the same, except for the red hearts or the Christmas decorations that overflow the cities, there is no difference with any other day.

Do you love your loved ones more that day? No, you love them exactly the same, but on that day, you pay more attention to these emotions.

There is not one day you have a birthday, you don´t go from being 41 to 42 on the exact day of your birthday, it is something that happens continuously throughout the year and your birthday is simply when the number changes.

Every time you consider a day of the year special, beautiful and romantic, you are saying that all other days are not. This means that you do not have the freedom to decide for yourself how to make a day special, but you have to wait for life to do it for you.

So how much are you in charge of your life, if one calendar day makes you feel so bad and tells you what to do?

The real reason to celebrate any of these special days should be the celebration that you are alive, the gratitude towards your parents and loved ones, the enjoyment of love and friendship, but again, why limit yourself on doing it only that calendar day and not the whole year or when you decide to do it?

You shouldn't wait for a specific day to express your love, affection and gratitude, but rather make sure that your loved ones feel it constantly and take care of them all year long.

If a day on the calendar makes you suffer, the solution is to take away the importance from that day, because no day is more special than another. You have the power to decide which moments of your life are special and which are not, when to celebrate and when not to. Take charge of your life!

If all the days of the year are the same and any day is good to take care of your loved ones and celebrate, then February 14, Christmas, birthdays are good too. Celebrate these days if you can and feel like it, but not because you have to. Play down the special days and just enjoy and celebrate life whenever you can.

Finally, remember that if you don't want to celebrate any of these days, you don't have to, you are free. Nobody, not even your family or any system or social commitment has power over you. If a date makes you nostalgic or sad, eliminate the idea that it is a special day. Remember: for dogs and plants it's just another normal and ordinary day.

Satisfaction in Life

My life is simple, I am happy.

The word satisfaction means "to satisfy a passion or need." Satisfaction doesn't have to do with the experience of Joy but with the experience of non-suffering, which is completely different. It's one thing to do something for Joy and another thing is to do it to stop suffering. For example, one thing is looking for a partner because you want to live the experience of love and another thing is looking for a partner because it hurts too much to be alone.

The need for satisfaction arises from suffering for a lack of something. It's this lack or absence that makes you suffer and feel unsatisfied in different aspects of your life and what leads you to feel that you have needs. This is why you hope to feel satisfied when your salary increases, when you have the house of your dreams, when you have a partner, when you have children, etc. It doesn't matter if you achieve your goals or not, you never feel satisfied in most cases, and in others, satisfaction lasts only a few days or weeks.

Then you look for new goals and objectives to satisfy that need in an endless cycle. This is how Greed is born.

The solution is not to create new goals every time you feel unsatisfied, but find the origin of that lack or absence within yourself, in order to dissolve the cause. A disease must not be hidden, but rather studied, analyzed and cured. Then you can distinguish if your desire is born from joy and wanting to improve in life, or from greed.

Take a minute and honestly think about something you need, allow yourself to be free, even materialistic, the only thing that matters right now is to think about those needs. You got them?

Well, about what you thought, the reality is that you don't need that, because if they were real needs as such, you would be dead now for not having them. So, it is not a need but a desire. When you realize that you don't need that, you will feel a knot in your stomach, that is the discomfort that pushes you to greed and makes you feel unsatisfied. The only things you really need in life are food, clothes, shelter and to breathe. Realize that all your needs right now are covered. At this very moment you only need to breathe, so take a deep breath realizing that you truly have everything you need.

So how difficult is life? You just have to breathe!

True satisfaction is born from returning to simplicity, this is what allows you to open yourself to gratitude. Gratitude, because at this very moment you don't need anything to survive. The rest are luxuries and extras, but you already have the essential and basic.

Take a deep breath and let yourself feel this emotion of satisfaction and fulfillment. If you accept it, you will realize that you are protected, as if wrapped or held, just as when as a child your mother held you in her arms and took care of you. This experience of protection and care is known in almost all religions as the Divine Mother who protects us.

Maybe something inside of you doesn't agree and feels this is not enough, that's the problem to be healed, that's the greed that actually keeps you from creating and achieving your goals and objectives.

Suppose you have a friend you give several gifts to, but never thanks you and is always dismissive. After some time, would you still want to give this friend a gift? Most likely not. However, if another friend with every gift, no matter how small or insignificant, gets excited, smiles and thanks you, then you're going to want to keep taking care of this friend, right?

In the same way, if you say to life through your actions, thoughts and emotions "it's not enough, I don't like this, I want more", metaphorically, nature decides not to give you anything else, it's what we call Karma. But if you live in a constant state of gratitude, simplicity and satisfaction, knowing and feeling that you don't need anything more than what you already have, that everything else is an extra and it will be fantastic whether it happens or not, then nature says "here, have a little more and a little more." Now your life will begin to improve exponentially.

Greed is the disease. Gratitude, satisfaction, feeling protected and cared for in the arms of the Divine Mother, the medicine. Feel and express gratitude.

To develop gratitude and satisfaction, I recommend the following meditation:
Krutaña Ayata MajaShakti (pronounced as it is written) means "Thank you for the overabundance that I already have great Mother." Take about 5-10 minutes a day repeating this mantra every few seconds in your mind, as you contemplate and remember that you have everything you need to live, feeling satisfaction and gratitude for your life as it is.

Then go out and work hard, strive to achieve your goals and objectives, but not from greed but from the desire to evolve, to be better, from gratitude and you will see you'll achieve your goals.

Krutana Ayata MajaShakti

Do you dare to be a Saint?

*Your attitude and behavior can make
a difference in humanity, if you wish.*

Society is not ready to have Saints; however, humanity needs them. Do
you dare to be one?

What does it mean to be a Saint? It depends on the definition each one
gives to the word. Here we use the explanation most commonly used in
many traditions such as Catholicism, Hinduism, Buddhism, and
Kabbalah.

A Saint is a virtuous person. Someone who through spiritual practice
(whatever the path), develops the virtues to the point of becoming those
virtues. Virtue is no longer what they do, but what they are.

These virtues are behaviors and states of being that lead to the end of
their own and other people's suffering, such as: Forgiveness,
Compassion, Peace, Gratitude, Hope, Faith, Humility, Justice, Charity,
Prudence, etc.

A Saint is a servant of God / Amitabha / Brahma ... and that doesn't
mean that saints should leave their job and dedicate to pray. Some do it
and that's fine, but we also need "holy spies" to infiltrate companies,
society, hospitals, politics, among the rich and among the poor, between
the healthy and the sick, among your own family. And from within, be
able to radiate and inspire those virtuous behaviors, generating a
tremendously profound butterfly effect on the whole humanity.

A Saint is a person who brings Peace where apparently there are conflicts;
who never hesitates to forgive everyone even those who don't know how
to forgive; who feels compassion towards those who have no compassion;
who loves those who don't know how to love; someone who has more
faith than pride; who has more hope than greed; who is fair rather than
envious.

A saint is one who even when faced and attacked by their worst enemy, their gaze, words and actions only sustain and express compassion, forgiveness, peace and love. That's a Saint.

So again, do you dare to be a Saint?

If your answer is yes, don't wait to be a Saint to act like one. Get started today. Forgive your fellows and your enemies. Love your neighbor. Promote Peace rather than conflict, feel Gratitude for life as it is right now. Then you will be walking the Holy Path.

And if your answer is no, you are loved anyway.

Interlude: The 4 Noble Truths

(1) There is suffering in life. It is inevitable, you must accept that sometimes you suffer. This is the first step to then (2) understand the origin of your pain. Once you know the origin of suffering, you are ready to (3) walk the path to its liberation. Have faith and hope, walk through it so you can finally discover that the suffering is gone, (4) there is no suffering.

Part 2: Ahamkara

Ahamkara means "ego" in Sanskrit and refers to your individuality and your actions as a human being. This second part is focused on understanding yourself and how your ego works. It is the moment of self-discovery.

What is ego?

Your ego and you are the same thing. Don't fight it, make it your best friend.

Ego is a Latin word that means "I". From many points of view, it has been defined as a part of human beings, to which all our negative reactions and our suffering are attributed. Based on this, many contemplate that we must end the ego and destroy it to free ourselves. But this is a misunderstanding of what ego is and how it works, and this confusion can sometimes lead to self-hatred.

The ego is innate, not only in the human beings, but in any life form (animals, plants, etc.), since the ego is what provides individuality. You cannot separate the ego from you or from any life form because they are not two different things, you are your ego and your ego is you.

In practically all religions and philosophies it is contemplated, in short, how a light, energy or universal consciousness became densified to the point of becoming individual, becoming the soul (Higher Self or I Am) and thus allowing incarnation in a human body. The ego is precisely the mechanism that allows that consciousness, which is still universal, to become an individual being, what we call "I". Hence, insects, plants and animals also have a kind of ego, since it´s what allows their tangibility. Of course, then the behavior of this ego varies in each life form depending on different factors that are now not important.

So, the ego is really what allows us to be here, incarnated, living the life that we live. It´s what keeps us alive and what protects us.

Metaphorically, your ego is like your computer's antivirus. The purpose of the antivirus is to make sure that nothing attacks, infects or destroys your computer. Now imagine for a moment that the antivirus gets out of control and begins to control which programs to run, which files to open and what to delete, that would be really problematic. The solution is not to remove the antivirus because you need it; the solution is to "educate" the antivirus so that it understands that its job is only to protect and that you, as a conscience, are in charge.

You cannot kill your ego no matter how much you want. When you hear someone says "I have no ego", in fact it is their ego speaking! None of the great masters of history like Buddha, Jesus, Krishna, Melkitzedeq, Maha Vajra, etc., claimed to be free of ego. Instead, everyone said and taught that we have to understand, educate, and make it our best friend and ally. Even so, stay in charge of yourself not as an ego, but as a Soul or the higher Consciousness that you also are.

How do you educate your ego?

To train a puppy dog, what you usually do is give him a treat when he pees in the newspaper and punish him when it does it on the couch. After several times, the dog finally understands and prefers to pee in the newspaper to receive the treat and avoid punishment. Your ego is not intelligent by itself; it is very instinctive and animalistic. Only understands cause and effect, like pets.

So, consider this: if one day you are sad or depressed and decide to eat chocolate because you feel bad, after doing it so many times, what do you think your ego will do when it feels like chocolate? Exactly, causing you a depression because that is the way to get it. Every time you go shopping, eat chocolate or drink a beer because you feel bad, first of all, that doesn´t solve your discomfort and second, you are rewarding your ego for that suffering and saying "very well done, keep on doing it like this".

The next time you feel bad, don't run for the reward directly, you don't deserve it, you haven't earned it yet. Instead, do this exercise and take at least a few minutes to meditate, pray, do therapy, or any spiritual practice, even if it's only 3-5 minutes. And at the end of the spiritual practice, you take the reward and say to yourself out loud: "This chocolate is not because of depression, but because of the meditation and therapy we just did, very well done" and then you eat it. It will seem absurd, but it really works because the moment you say it, your ego relates the reward to your spiritual practice and not to depression or discomfort. Do it so many times and you will see how suddenly your ego is going to be telling you "meditate, pray, do something spiritual please!"

With this simple exercise you will be turning the ego into your best friend and, instead of trying to sabotage you and prevent your spiritual and life evolution, it will help you achieve all your goals, whatever they may be.

Hate your ego and you will be hating yourself.
Love your ego and you will be loving yourself.
You are your ego.

Farewell to anger attacks

You are not angry, you are disappointed.

Anger, rage and wrath are common in everyday life, they happen due to stress and worries. Feeling that discomfort is unpleasant and you often don't know what to do. In order to dissolve it, you must study what causes it and how it works.

Anger is the accumulation of frustrations, rage and disappointments within us that, not knowing how to handle them, join together until it is too big and beats you.

It's like a time bomb, all that pressure is inside you until someone presses the button and detonates it. The problem is that every time it explodes, you splash your surroundings, hurting other people, and then you feel guilty and sorry. On the other hand, if instead of projecting it on the outside, you make the decision to repress so as not to hurt anyone, then you hurt yourself by punching tables, walls, or because of the internal pressure, you generate dissatisfaction, apathy for life and, as it gets bigger, ends up generating diseases such as heart attacks or cancer.

If you project it outside, you hurt others, if you keep it inside, you hurt yourself. What to do then? The most obvious solution is not to get angry, however, this is not a decision we can make, or at least not for the moment. Remember every time you got angry; you didn't choose it. You don't decide to get angry at your children, partner, at work or with the car that ran into you, it happens because of the pressure inside of you. The more personal growth and spirituality you do, the more you have a chance not to get angry. In the meantime, learn some tips so you can get rid of that anger without hurting anyone, not even yourself.

Some therapies recommend you to shout while being alone or punch a pillow to get the anger off your chest. Give 2 or 3 good screams (without hurting your throat) in your room or office alone, with loud music not to disturb others, or give two or three punches to a pillow (something soft that won't hurt yourself) will help you certainly. But you must remember that it's like a bomb, which means that once it exploded, there is no way back. You shouldn't keep screaming or punching the pillow for more than a minute, because from then on it is only drama and, far from helpful, it is leading you to remain in discomfort and the drama of life.

Once you have detonated the bomb in a controlled way, realize that you are projecting that rage and anger on someone, a situation or life; you are blaming the outside. But that person you project on is just the last straw that broke the camel's back. Your anger is inside you, not outside, it's you who feels it and it's you who can and should resolve it. No one is going to ease your anger. So, take a deep breath and agree to take charge of that anger by setting the people involved aside.

The next step is to pay attention to that anger and realize that behind it is disappointment. Accept that this situation or person disappointed you. Breathe and feel it. You are not angry, you are disappointed. Breathe. You are disappointed when someone lies, cheats, betrays, opposes you or don't do things the way you want.

Behind all the anger and outbursts, there is only disappointment. Accept the disappointment and you will see the anger and rage dissolve. Thus, instead of detonating the bomb, you disarm it without any explosion, therefore, without any damage.

Feeling disappointed is much healthier than anger and when you accept this, you are already on the road to recovery. Now, to dissolve disappointment you have to let go of the expectations that you constantly create in your life. Nobody can do things the way you do because you are unique, and you must understand and accept that each one has their own point of view and their way of doing things that may be different from yours, but not necessarily wrong. Stop placing your expectations on others, no one has been created to satisfy you or to be at your service, just as you are not here to serve anyone. We all collaborate with each other in the best way we can and at our own understanding.

When you finally let go of your anger and expectations then joy can arise. There is something in common between joy and anger: the energy is the same. If you notice, anger explodes exactly like a big laugh, an explosion of joy or the satisfaction of an orgasm. Notice that at times you got angry and immediately laughed at what happened. The difference between anger and joy is that in anger there is no awareness and in joy there is.

The next time you feel rage or anger, remember: you are not angry but disappointed. Then remain aware of that disappointment and expectations. Finally contemplate the word *Sukhi* (it means "joy") and you will see how that anger is transformed by happiness. Meditate daily on *Sukhi* and your internal joy will increase exponentially, needing less and less from the outside.

Self-esteem

I am who I am and it is fine that way.

Self means "toward self" and esteem means "to appreciate or value". Therefore, self-esteem is the value of oneself, it's how you perceive yourself. In reality, it doesn't have to do with what others think or say about you, but with what you think about yourself, this is why the prefix *self*.

The difference between having a high or low self-esteem depends on the eye of the beholder. Those who look at themselves and only see their defects, the things they do wrong, their mistakes, insecurities, etc., feel that they have no self-esteem. For them It's common not to pay attention to what they master and do well, they deny that completely, and even when someone close to them highlights these aspects, they dismiss them as if they were trifles. Low self-esteem is closely related to being pessimistic.

Remember for example when a friend took you to a brand store you didn't know before and you loved it. Before that day you didn't even know that brand existed, but from that moment on you realized that a lot of your friends used it and that even on the street you always walk through there are one or two of those stores that you've never seen. That brand store was always there, you just didn't realize it because it didn't enter your field of perception, until someone showed it to you. You function this way in life, you perceive and see only what is within your field of physical perception, but also within your mental and emotional fields.

Being pessimistic is just looking at the negative, for example, negative people see a car skip a traffic light and get angry and upset about how badly people drive, but don't see the previous 100 cars that didn't roll the stoplight, because it doesn't enter their field of perception. Pessimists live life from hell because everything is pain and suffering, but the reality is that they are the ones denying the other part of the story. In the same way, low self-esteem is being pessimistic but about yourself, it is only looking at the negative and denying the other part.

When you think you don't have self-esteem, you try to overcompensate by going to the other extreme, the so-called high self-esteem. This is just the opposite: completely denying your flaws, your shortcomings and looking only at the best in you, the things that you are good at and all your good skills and abilities. And when something negative about you comes up, you immediately look at a good aspect to make up for it. It is orienting your field of perception only on how good you are, therefore, forcing yourself to be optimistic.

If the pessimist denies cars that respect the stoplight, the optimist denies cars that skip it. Therefore, this excess of positivism makes you live in the clouds without having your feet on the ground and without being able to solve the difficulties and problems you face. Furthermore, this alleged high self-esteem is tremendously easy to break; You only need someone to show you your flaws and defects and your self-esteem will be completely destroyed, and you will have to build it again.

As you can see, both extremes sooner or later are going to make you suffer. What can we do then?

A great solution is to remove self-esteem from the equation, stop considering whether you have it or not, because now you know that it is just the way you perceive yourself. To be able to do this, you have to accept that there are some aspects and areas that you are very good at and others you are not so good. This is normal, there is nothing wrong with that, it happens to all of us. For example, if you are bad at math, driving, public speaking or whatever, it does not mean that you are a bad person or completely incompetent, it just means that in those areas you are not good and you are only incompetent there but not as a human being. Don't allow yourself to judge the totality of yourself only from your limitations. Don't allow yourself to be ashamed, as we all have flaws. Math experts might laugh at you because you take time to calculate a tip, but then maybe they don't know anything about art, fashion or music and you do. Everyone judges others from what they do know and assume that everyone should know, but at the same time they have their own limitations, inadequacies and insecurities in other fields.

If you grab a bottle of water and yell "orange juice!", Did the water turn into orange juice? No, the water always stays as water no matter what anyone says. Likewise, someone calling you incompetent or dumb doesn't makes you that, and this includes when you are the one calling yourself that. Your opinion of yourself doesn't change the reality of who you are.

Learn to be objective with yourself, look at all aspects of your life and accept those you're good at, as well as those that you're not. Do not exaggerate either of them, be objective and you will see that you trust yourself in many more aspects than you don't. It may be difficult for you to start noticing the positive aspects while your mind is on the negatives, but have a strong will and force yourself. You can even ask a friend for help, not to flatter you, but to help you open your field of perception about yourself, to introduce you to that brand store of yours that you still don't know. Then, contemplating both aspects, you can take a deep breath and repeat aloud "I accept myself as I am, I trust myself." Do it for about 5 minutes a day until you have developed that self-confidence.

This is how to develop great confidence, looking at yourself completely, enjoying everything you do well and accepting to strive and improve those aspects that you don't master, without being hard on yourself.

Don't develop self-esteem, remove it from your mind and your concepts, develop trust and pure honesty with yourself instead. This trust is now unshakeable because it is based on the truth of the totality of who you are.

Always remember that you are the water and not what anyone, including you, says about it.

Love your body

Don't do to yourself what you wouldn't do to others.
I love myself just the way I am.

The standards of beauty constantly change over time. Apparently, these changes have to do with trends, however, fashion and the conception of beauty are totally linked to the survival of humanity as a species. For example, between the 1400s and 1500s, obese women were a trend, being "fat" was beautiful. Why? At that time there was famine, people ate what they could to survive, so being fat meant that, not only did you have enough to survive, but you also had enough to eat luxury or abundant food. It was synonymous with wealth and well-being; therefore, it became attractive, it was beautiful. At that time, people didn't worry about lengthening life expectancy, but about surviving one more day.

Today there is no famine in most countries and we even choose what to eat and how much. We are not concerned now with surviving the present day, but with expanding life expectancy and having the best possible health for old-age. This is why having excess body fat now has become something "ugly", because that excess fat can shorten your life or worsen your health and comfort in old age. The human being and therefore society have an innate survival instinct, which makes all the features that will ensure our existence become fashionable. By becoming a trend, everyone will want to be in, pushing people towards survival and better health.

This helps us to expand the perception of beauty, but above all, it is useful to free ourselves from some pressures. Most people are not satisfied with their body, it doesn't matter if they are top models, if they are in good shape, or if they are obese, the reality is that they don't accept their body or some parts of it.

Surely you have a friend who, in your opinion, has a good body and is continually complaining in disapproval, despite looking good. Maybe you are that person complaining!

Trying to pretend or convince yourself that you are not interested in those canons doesn't work, because you still feel equally guilty about looking at yourself in the mirror and knowing that you don't fit in. The solution is to learn to love you as you are.

To do this, consciously observe that hatred and self-rejection while you breathe, until you can understand and feel that you did not choose the color of your eyes, your height, the shape of your nose, the size of your breasts or genitals. Your metabolism has a tendency to gain weight or lose weight. Understand that none of this was your choice. So, you haven't done anything wrong, it wasn't your decision, it just happened. You have done nothing wrong. You have been fighting your own nature for too long and suffering for how you look, aren't you already tired? Stop being hard on yourself, stop punishing yourself. Your body is perfect just the way it is.

Every time you complain about your appearance, every time you reject yourself for how you look, you are hurting yourself. Your body feels rejected and literally becomes depressed because it only receives negativity and hatred. You would never think to approach a person and for 15 minutes insult them by telling them how ugly or fat they look, right? You wouldn't because you know you'd hurt that person so much. So why are you doing it to yourself in front of the mirror? That is not compassionate to you, the same harm you would do to that person you're doing to yourself. Breathe.

If you are objective, you'll see that it is not the totality of your body that you don't like, it's only the envelope. Notice that your lungs take care of you by breathing without having to do anything. Your heart beats constantly to make sure you are still alive and all your internal organs take care of you 24 hours a day from when you were born until today without a single break. So, the truth is that you love and like 95% of your body, everything that is inside and works well, but you only look at the 5% of the envelope and the body fat and from there, you judge the totality dramatizing.

Now looking at it from another perspective, think about something you like a lot in your life, perhaps a sport, cinema, music, some food, sexuality or enjoying your family. Remember the happiness you feel when doing these activities. It is thanks to your body that you can live these experiences. Your body is what allows you to enjoy life. This is more than enough reason to love your body.

Accept your body as it is. Love yourself and then do some exercise, eat a balanced diet, make sure you are in good health and be responsible so that you have the best possible quality of life.

Take about 6 minutes a day, the first 3 minutes let yourself consciously feel that hatred and rejection, breathing to allow all the pressure to come off. Then for the last 3 minutes observe and feel your body and repeat in your mind: "I love myself as I am. *"Prema"*. *Prema* means love in Sanskrit. When you repeat it by feeling your body, you are saying to your body "I love you". Repeat this exercise daily for 21 days and you will discover the big difference.

Value or not Value?

I have no value; I don't lack value. I just am.

Doctors, lawyers, architects, etc., are considered by many to be important people. Sometimes even they consider themselves special and better, with a higher value, and they look down on peasants, workers, street cleaners. However, you need an architect once in your life or perhaps never directly, you will need a lawyer a couple of times in your life, just as to a doctor. But how often do you need the farmer, sweeper or cleaner? Every day; a single day without farmers and the supermarkets would be empty bringing chaos to society.

One day without cleaning the streets and bad smells and hygiene would become a very serious problem in the cities. A day without cleaning the bathroom of your business can cost you many unsatisfied customers. So, who is more valuable, the graduated architect or the uneducated farmer? If in your mind you answered the farmer, you are wrong, the correct answer is both equally, because without architects we would not have firm homes to live in, without lawyers, society would not know how to relate and respect each other, and without doctors, we would die from a simple flu. Without them, society would be in complete chaos, just as without farmers, ranchers, cleaners, office workers, plumbers, electricians, etc.

Each person establishes in their mental system what is important in life and what is not from their point of view, and condition their judgment about the value of people according to their decision. This makes you appreciate some people or positions and discredit those who do not fulfill your success standards. Maybe one day you made fun of someone's job and the next day you were in need of their services because you are incompetent in that area.

There is no job more dignified or with more value or importance than another, if you get paid for what you do, your work is necessary as much as any other, otherwise they wouldn't pay you for it. So, you shouldn't be ashamed for what you do because you are contributing to the welfare of society in one way or another.

This causes, for example, that everyone wants to charge a lot for the work they do, and want to pay very little (or better still nothing) for the work, effort and knowledge of others. Think about how often and easily you consider the price an electrician or plumber charges you for their services to be expensive; you immediately think they want to cheat or abuse you. Before making that judgment, you must consider that, if everywhere you are given the same price, then it´s not expensive, it´s what it costs. Then you must consider their effort and work, such as traveling to your home, going to buy spare parts, then doing the repair again and generally everything urgently. The question you should ask yourself is: If I did that job, how much would I like to charge? Then you most likely understand how much they charge you.

The Value thus becomes something totally subjective, purely based on the comparison of what each one considers important and of your capability with respect to others. If in the field in which you compare yourself you are good, you win and then you feel valuable, but if you lose, you feel worthless and you make the other one valuable.

The reality is that value doesn´t exist. We are all the same. Absolutely everyone comes from the same "place" (God, Light, origin, consciousness or whatever you want to call it). If everything in the world were made of stones, the word "stone" would have no meaning because it would be the only thing that exists. If we all come from the same place, it means that we all have exactly the same value, therefore, nobody has value and nobody lacks it.

The solution not to struggle to prove your worth or suffer for not having it, is to eliminate the value of the equation. Let go completely of the question of value and self-importance, and accept with simplicity and humility those aspects of life in which you are efficient, as well as those in which you are not. Accept both sides without even considering value as a possibility. Then you discover that you have no value, but you also lack value. You live completely in the middle and there is nothing and no one to get you out of there.

I have no value; I don't lack value. I just am, we just are.

You are the source of your true happiness

Facing your suffering it's the gateway to joy.

When we start a spiritual path, one of the questions that always comes up is about happiness, what it is and how to achieve it.

Happiness and Joy in your life have been temporary. One day you are happy, because you have a new job; another day you are happy because you are on vacation; then you are happy because it's your birthday; you are happy because you have a partner or because you have children or because, because, because... you are always looking for a reason to be happy, until you reach a point where you put happiness aside and only look for the reason, instead of Joy itself.

And it happens that life is constantly showing you that these reasons were not a permanent cause of your happiness, but only temporary and ephemeral. Then suddenly in the new job you get upset because you work 3 more hours; you are sad because your vacation is over; you get depressed because your partner left you; you feel alone because your children became emancipated or because, because, because... So, the same reason that made you feel happy at a certain point, in time becomes the reason that generates exactly the same amount of suffering as the previous happiness. Then you say: "Oh, I have to find another job, another partner, have more children, I need more vacations or I want a dog ..." and you just have fallen into the same vicious circle. Does it sound familiar to you?

Given this, the solution is not to leave your job, partner or children. Of course not, that would be fleeing from the reality in which you live, isolating yourself and finally you will suffer more from the repression. What you have to do, is eliminate the reasons, stop fighting. Understand that life has been constantly showing you that you cannot be in a permanent state of Joy if you continue to look for it only outside. This has a bright side: it means that if permanent happiness is not found on the outside, then you have to look for it within you. It is the only place where perhaps you have not looked for it yet!

Here is a very simple, incredibly effective and powerful exercise. Put all your intention and willpower, go beyond shame and do it: Begin to imagine how each of your cells turns into a smiley face, imagine how each cell smiles at the next and the next one smiles back. Little by little, your whole body turns into smiley faces, everything is smiling, your muscles are made up of big and ridiculous smiley faces, your bones cry with laughter, your nervous system sends smiley faces throughout your body, you only think of smiles and joy ... and now bring those smiley faces to your face. Smile! Bigger, even if you don't feel like it, even if it costs, take out your maximum willpower, force yourself and... Smiiiiileeeeeeeeeee!!!

Take a deep breath, relax your body, and let go of the contemplation.

If you did it, you must have felt at least a little joy. What was the reason? What was the motive? None, you only thought and focused on Joy and it arose spontaneously. AHA! You have just verified that Joy and Happiness are really already within you. You are your own source of joy and happiness. And now you know how to feel them.

If joy is already within us, how is it that we are not always in that state? Imagine for a second that I give you a box of oranges and when you open it, you discover that there are 5 or 6 rotten ones, what is the first thing you would do? You'd probably take out the rotten ones because you know if you don't, they're all going to end up the same. You'd never dream of emptying the box, putting the rotten ones in the bottom and putting all the healthy ones on top and saying "Now, they're all healthy," would you?

Metaphorically, that box is you and the oranges are your emotions. Throughout your life, many problems or conflicts have happened so that inside you there are rotten emotions and healthy emotions mixed, so the question is what are you waiting to remove the rotten ones?

Trying to force Joy by denying what makes you feel bad, is equivalent to hiding the rotten oranges at the bottom of the box and saying "this doesn't affect me." Joy is a natural state of Being, it is always there, what happens is that there are so many rotten oranges that we forget that happiness has always been inside, deep down. The solution is to remove negative emotions, dissolve everything that makes us suffer. What will be left in the box when you have removed the rotten oranges? Only the healthy ones, the beautiful ones, that is to say: Joy, Happiness, Calm; Or in other words, your true essence, what you are really made of: your Soul, your Consciousness, your Divinity. Breathe.

Each of the negative emotions that you have felt or feel in your life are there to teach you something, so that you can evolve. When all goes well, you settle in, relax, and don't move, then after a break, life gives you a nudge to remind you to keep moving forward.

Think how many times thanks to the fact that your boss, client, parents, partner, etc. scolded you, you realized that you had to change something and you evolved, and in the end, you even were thankful for that. When you receive a push, it is up to you to accept it as the beginning of a movement, of a new evolution, or to fight against and turn it into a real pitched battle of years.

How to dissolve negative emotions and take hidden learning? Through attention. Consciousness is the solvent of suffering. You must pay conscious attention to that pain, without denying it, but also not dramatizing it; observe and feel it with severity and objectivity. To help you stay conscious, consider these 4 steps or states:

1) Breathe: think about the emotion you want to eliminate and breathe from your abdomen.
2) Inhabit: open the door to that emotion, let it enter you, let it dwell your body rather than reject or fight it.

3) Feel: feel that emotion now, without trying to change it, without drama. Just pay attention to it, stay aware of that suffering as long as it takes while you breathe from the abdomen.
4) Observe: see how your discomfort is diminishing and finally disappearing.

Every time some suffering is released, there is an empty space where that negative emotion used to be, so it is time to fill our box with new oranges, that is, to put Joy within us. So again, you must repeat the exercise of "Smiley Faces". Some suffering has been released; it is time to celebrate!

There are people who like mantras and the use of *malas* (traditional necklaces of 108 beads), if that is your case, you can also chant the mantra of Joy:

Sukhi Ananda Ram
Sukhi = Joy
Ananda = Blessing
Ram = Higher, intense and present pleasure

This mantra means something like: "I am aware of all Joy, Blessing and Pleasure." You can create a link with this mantra so that the energy of Joy flows through your body and into your life with ease and intensity. To do this, you must repeat it for about 25 minutes a day for 12 consecutive days or, if you use a *mala*, you will do 9 *malas* a day for 12 consecutive days. From day 12, whenever you feel like, sing it, enjoy it and live it.

Smile and always remember, everything's fine!

You are Free, Take your place in life!

My place is where I am, my place is me here and now.

All human beings are free, yet there is a difference between Freedom and Anarchy. Anarchy is the belief that we can do whatever we want regardless of the consequences or other people, that is not freedom. Being free means that you have every right to do whatever you want whenever you want, but never keeping others from that same freedom and without hurting anyone along the way.

If someone has to suffer for you to achieve a goal, or it is not a good goal, or it is not the best way to achieve it. It becomes anarchy and self-centeredness; it is not freedom. For example, if you like sarcastic humor, it means that to laugh someone has to suffer; If to encourage your sports team you need to insult others, is that a good way to do it? Think about it, how do you feel when they laugh at you, when they insult you or when they don't respect you? That's what others feel when you act that way. There are always options to laugh, to have a good time, to achieve your goals without hurting anyone, so everyone enjoys it, everyone benefits.

Everyone seeks a full life; however, it's not possible if in their efforts to achieve it they do not include others. Self-centeredness limits your happiness and peace, and in the end, you always end up feeling guilty. Sharing and including others in your actions makes you feel good, it makes you happy to see everyone's satisfaction, including yours.

Just as you mustn't impose your freedom on others, you mustn't allow others to impose their freedom on you. What does this mean? Sometimes your actions can hurt others and you should do everything you can to avoid it, but sometimes you did the right thing and others suffered from their own expectations. For example, suppose you make a decision that only concerns you, such as changing jobs, cities or partners, and your mother is disappointed by your decision and says the typical "you're making me suffer." In such a situation, it's not you who is hurting your mother, she is hurt by her expectations and her attachments, and she is trying to impose her freedom on yours. You must not allow it; you must take your power and reaffirm yourself. If you don't, you end up living according to what others say or think, and you lose control of your life by giving it to others. Learn to differentiate when your actions or decisions cause suffering to others and when they suffer for their own reasons. If something concerns you and your life only, it´s s not someone else's business and no one has the right to comment on it.

Understanding this difference is the first step in taking your place and power in life. For a long time, you have been trying to get your place from your parents, your partners, your children, friends, bosses, etc., and you have fought hard to make it happen. You have done everything you can to show everyone and yourself that you are good enough and that you deserve a place in life, in your family and at work. And after all those efforts, nobody has given you your place in life. It's frustrating, right?

The reason why no one has given you your place until now and they will never do, is because they don't have it. Therefore, no one can give you something they don't have. Your place in life is in you, here and now, you are the one who decides whether to take it or not. When you don't take it, it remains empty, nobody takes it up for you, nobody takes it away from you. Don't ask anyone for permission, not even yourself: don't wait for your ego to agree to do it. Take your place and your power, it´s your responsibility. Accept that you exist, that you have the right to life. Just do it and live.

Realize how many things you want to do and don't do because of fear of what they may think of you or because you think you don't deserve it. How many opportunities have you already let go of in life? Do you feel good to see them pass in front of you and not act? Think of something you want ... well, you are entitled to that experience. To achieve it perhaps you will have to make an effort, but you must go for it, just make sure not to hurt anyone on the way and not to fall into anarchy or recklessness.

If you want to eat ice cream, a chocolate bar or a hamburger, do it without feeling guilty, enjoy it. Nobody dies for it, just be wise to take care of your health, eat healthy and do some exercise, but do it. If you want to buy a shirt and you have the money, you don't have to wait for your birthday to buy it. You have the right to do so, be prudent, don´t spend what you don´t have. If you like a person, don't hide your feelings, you have the right to love, sex, and fun. Go for what you want. Do not flee from life and its experiences but rather embrace it, throw yourself into it wisely, but definitely living it.

Don´t expect anyone to give you permission to be happy, you are the only responsible for achieving it. Do you want to go to the movies, to have dinner or to dance and don´t have with whom? Go alone, there is nothing shameful about it, it´s your right to life and your emancipation, and what others think about it is not your problem, it doesn´t concern you.

You already know what a life of repression, conditioning and frustration is. Now is the time for emancipation, to take your place and understand life. "My place is where I am, it´s what I am, I am alive and now I live."

Meditating for 5 to 10 minutes a day on the word *Swasthya* (it is pronounced suastia), which means "I am self-contained" in Sanskrit, will make you realize that you are self-sufficient and that you already have everything you need to do what you want. and therefore, you will be able to take your power and place in a peaceful but decisive way.

The Feminine Essence

Be independent and autonomous but never lose your femininity.

Tara, Lakshmi, Mary or Mother Earth. Throughout the existence of humanity, the female figure has always played a fundamental role. In every religion there is a name for that feminine energy, which is generally known as Divine Mother or Universal Mother. But what is it and how does it affect us?

Let's use an example. Suppose you live in Chiapas. Chiapas is in Mexico. Mexico is on the American Continent and this one on planet Earth. The Earth in the Solar System and the Solar System in the Universe. Where is the Universe? In the Divine Mother.

Metaphorically, to prepare a broth you need the pot to contain it; In the same way, for the universe to exist, a universal container is needed, this is what we call the Matrix of the Divine Mother.

This Divine Mother, therefore, is not a physical person but an attitude, an elevated energy or consciousness. She has the quality of caring for and protecting everything that is inside her, like a mother who cares for and protects her baby and her family. It's also who provides food in the form of consciousness and energy, just as a mother feeds through the umbilical cord and the milk from her breasts. It's also the one that always accompanies you, no matter what is happening, to ease loneliness, cuddle you and fill you with love, just like a mother holds her child in her loving arms.

This energy is not exclusive to women, but it is also inside men, it is present in everyone in a different way and each person must learn to find it, accept it and use it appropriately.

Women are a direct incarnation of this Divine or Universal Mother, so they generally possess the qualities of caring innately, effortlessly. However, throughout history and mainly due to *machismo*, these features are sometimes misinterpreted and judged as a symbol of weakness and inferiority. This has created a confusion between the rights of women-men, and between the nature and essence of each gender.

Women and men have the same rights in terms of legality and society. Men are not superior to women, nor are women superior to men. No man has the right to subdue a woman, nor vice versa. We have the same rights and yet we are different.

A man knows how to conquer a woman, but then it becomes difficult to take care of the relationship because of this limitation of feminine energy. A woman, on the other hand, has a hard time taking the first step and conquer a man, but she knows how to take care of him later. A man knows how to make money, but it is hard for him to save. A woman knows how to save.

We are different in our way of thinking and feeling, in that to which we give importance and no posture is better than the other, both are good. Peace between genders is achieved when both accept their own nature and then that of the opposite gender as it is, without judgment.

Women's search for independence is a wonderful thing. The problem is that, sometimes, to achieve this autonomy they do it through struggling against their own nature and / or against the other gender. They are convinced they do not need men in their lives, they don't have to take care of anyone, they can do everything alone, the famous quotes "all men are the same" or "who needs men". And what they are doing is losing their feminine essence by masculinizing. This later becomes the suffering of loneliness, of not having the support or a partner by their side to share their life with because they have lost that essence that makes them attractive as women.

Fulfilling yourself as a woman is not denying the feminine essence, but embracing who you are. Be independent, have a job, make your decisions according to your wishes and goals. Do not allow submission, give your opinion, but never lose your femininity. Never leave aside your ability to care, transmit love, protect, support. It is not incompatible. The more you accept these qualities, the easier and faster you will achieve your personal success. Make peace with yourself and your femininity.

For men, the exercise is to awaken this ability to care, give love and not only worry about the results, but also about the means. Understand that worrying about your emotions and those of your family doesn't make you less of a man. Know that no one has an obligation to take care of you and pamper you, therefore you cannot demand it, but accept when it happens and learn to take care of yourself. Finally, it is being conscious that the same care that you want to receive from a woman, others also want to receive it from you.

As a man, connecting with your Divine Mother will calm your aggressiveness, violence and the constant change of mind. It will allow you to be gentle with everyone, yet still decisive and clear in your goals and power.

To recover and increase that essence of the Universal Mother and the feminine energy in you both woman and man, I recommend this simple exercise: Breathe from your abdomen calmly and imagine that you are held in the arms of that Divine Mother (Mary, *Tara, Lakshmi* ...), like when you were little and your mother carried you, only now she is not your biological mother, but the Universal Mother. And for 5 or 10 minutes allow yourself to relax and surrender in her arms allowing her to fill you with peace and love. This will remove the feeling of emptiness and loneliness within you. Do this exercise every day for 15 days and you will feel much better about yourself.

Male Essence

Power is love, not violence.

Power. There is Power in the universe. It is the origin of creation; it's the Big Bang. And when power is pure, it's not an experience of violence or aggressiveness. Power doesn't corrupt nor is it greedy. It's the experience of embracing life with passion, of declaring that you're alive and acting decisively. It's remembering your divine essence and using it.

But there is something that prevents you, what is it? Every painful power experience you've ever had. Every time your parents abuse power over you because of their incompetence, every time a teacher at your school, or anyone with authority yelled at you or made you feel bad, they have generated your judgments about power keeping you from understanding it. And as a result, this has made it difficult for you to achieve your goals.

Think of a kitchen knife, you can use it to cut vegetables and make a delicious broth or in a fit of rage you can stick it to someone. The knife is just a tool, neither good nor bad; the use that you give to it will turn it into a kitchen tool or a weapon. The solution is not to throw your knives away to prevent you from attacking anyone, but to remain conscious and learn to use them to never hurt anyone including yourself. Your power is like this knife, it's just a mechanism, a universal principle you are entitled to and the use you give it will turn it into the energy to achieve and do what you want, or to try to harm and dominate others.

Sometimes you have projected that power against others by hurting them, other times someone projected it onto you and the result in both cases is that you blamed power for what happened. It's like throwing the knife at someone and blaming the knife. Power is not responsible or guilty for the damage you have caused or received, the responsibility lies with your incompetence or that of the other person to use it. You must forgive yourself and others for the misuse of power, practice and learn to use it in a compassionate way focused on your well-being and the well-being of others.

You must remember that you have no authority or power over anyone and no one has it over you. No one should suffer for your power nor you for someone else's. Just as you don't like to be imposed on, neither do others. To find this balance it's essential that the foundation of your power is love and not resentment or pride. Like a mother giving birth, where each contraction and push is an experience of power, full of love for her child.

When you connect with pure love, not conditioned by your control, disappointments or frustrations, but in its highest experience of freedom; when you have a deep desire to feel good about yourself and everyone else, to share that love, then your power emanates as an eternal, infinite and limitless source, capable of doing anything. It's the power of your *kundalini* under your control. It's an experience of celebration of life and existence, the declaration that you are that divine being and that you act as such.

This power is present in both men and women, so both must learn to take it and handle it from their own essences.

Men are the embodiment of this power, so they have more of this energy in their body and it's easier for them to take it and accept it. However, the problem for men is learning to use it from compassion and not falling into the extremes of aggressiveness or verbal or physical violence. You must understand that you should not project your power against anyone but use it in favor of yourself and others at the same time, remembering that all human beings have the same amount of power. And you must develop more compassion than pride.

This power in a man's body, is transformed into the desire to have a better life, to create goals and objectives, and to work to achieve them. But when this power is confused, it becomes the feeling of not being good enough providers and of having to do and produce more and more, and now men never feel satisfied with what they have achieved in life. A man who doesn't generate income, feels sad and depressed, because he feels worthless. It is thanks to this power that men improve and evolve, but taken to the extreme or obsession, it becomes a constant suffering from dissatisfaction. Then, men begin to compete for the best job, more money, the best partner, falling into greed and even violence to achieve it; they will misuse that power to prove their worth. When this happens, you need to remain aware of this instinctual drive so that you can calm it down and not get carried away by those feelings. You have nothing to prove to anyone, not even yourself. If in your life you do everything you can to be efficient and productive, you are doing it right, keep it up and don't be hard on yourself. Find your Pure Power, take it and then that need to prove yourself or not feeling good enough will disappear.

For women, developing this power can be a more difficult task, just as it is for men to develop feminine energy. It´s because feminine energy is so present in them that the masculine seems non-existent, but the reality is that it is only hidden and asleep. Just like when you are out of bread, you go out to the bakery to buy it, when you feel that something is missing inside you, you go outside to look for it. This is what causes men to seek out Divine Mothers and women to seek that power in men, trying to make up for what they feel is lacking in themselves. That is how they become codependents, convinced that what they want is outside, when it´s inside where they must find it.

When a woman doesn't feel that power within, she waits for someone else, usually a man, to take the first step for them. This first push is the power that women must awaken within, not expecting or taking for granted that someone will do it for you, understand that no one is going to save you.

You are the only responsible for your well-being and satisfaction. Awaken your power and take it, don´t look for it outside, it is in you. Be decisive towards your goals and go for them with this Pure Power. Do not confuse taking your power with going to the extreme of rejecting or fighting against men as sometimes happens. Remember that they don´t have your power, therefore, you don´t have to fight for it. You can perfectly take your power and still have a relationship.

Once men and women take their power, they feel whole and fulfilled again. This is the best condition to live together and interact with our partners, families, colleagues and friends. Full of Pure Power, intense, deep, based on love and compassion.

This mantra is recommended for both men and women, to connect with your power and learn to use it. Repeat 20 minutes a day for 12 days in a row *ShivaLingam,* this will help you accept the eternal and Divine Power that is in you.

One more step?

In spirituality and in life, you take one step after another at your own pace. However, every time you take one of those steps there is an internal fear. It is because you know what you know about yourself, but you still don't know what you have to discover. This is how the fear of the unknown appears, of what you may find on this path of self-knowledge.

This fear paralyzes you. Sometimes you are convinced that it is going to hurt to discover a new part of you that you have not yet resolved, other times there is guilt for having done something wrong and not remembering it, a senseless feeling of guilt. Certainly you don't know what you are going to find in that search and perhaps you have things to solve and unravel, but each step that you have taken has made you improve and feel good in the end, perhaps not during the purification process, but as a result. So, don't think about the process, let your ultimate inspiration be the wellbeing.

It is normal to feel you have opened Pandora's Box or the trunk of memories and in fact it is something like that, but don't let that stop you. You are in the process of change and purification. Looking at that box and thinking "I've still got a lot to integrate and solve!", is not the best attitude, as it makes you feel that you have a lot of work to do and it takes away your strength to take the next step.

As an example, think of what you are going to eat for your next meal today. Now think about everything you are going to eat tomorrow and the day after, and the next day. Think about the amount of food you are going to eat this whole year. If you imagine all that food in front of you thinking that you have to eat everything right now, would make you overwhelmed, and probably even lose your appetite. However, what you do is eat a little bit every day and you don't even realize how much you eat. You've been eating multiple times a day for years and you have never asked yourself "Wow! When will I be done eating for the rest of my life ...?" It doesn't make sense; you just eat when you're hungry. With spirituality and your evolution is the same thing. Imagine all you have to learn is like putting all the food you will eat in your entire life in front of you.

Be compassionate, there is no need to be hard on yourself. When you teach babies to walk and after taking a step they fall down, you don't look at them with contempt, you don't punish or judge them, but you pick them up and say "it's ok dear, try again." When they do it again and fall again, your answer is exactly the same, you never get angry at them for being incompetent at walking no matter how many times they fall. This is how you should look at yourself, every mistake you make is not actually a mistake, it's a step towards learning to walk. When you fall, God looks at you, grabs your hands and says "It's okay dear, try again" without judgment.

And when in any of those steps you discover something unresolved or painful about yourself, don't allow yourself to fall into pessimism and discard all the previous good work you have done. It is common after therapy or meditation for a long time, to reappear some old wound you thought was resolved (because there is still some point of view from which to observe it). Or maybe you get angry and your partner tells you "so much meditation and therapy and watch how you get", and at that moment you doubt everything you have worked on and resolved, believing that it has been in vain. Don't allow yourself to fall into that mistake. Every step you have taken and every issue you have solved, has been solved and has been a success, and now you just have to take that next step to solve the present issue, it's like your next meal. If the issue repeats itself, is that you are healing it from different points of view, do not despair, you're doing it right; have faith in evolution and in yourself.

Take one step at a time, give yourself a break between each step if you need or feel like it, and take the next step again when it's time to do it. Then you will no longer feel that you have things to solve or something to achieve, you will simply be taking the next step.

There is no goal to achieve or a mountain to climb in this life, but the next step to discover about ourselves. If life is always evolving, then as long as we are alive there will always be something to learn. Accept it and make peace with evolution, take one more step, just stay in the here and now and give the next step.

So, one more step?

Interlude: What you do and what you are

Before you had a first and last name, you already existed. Before you had studies or a job, you also existed. Therefore, you are not your name, nor your profession, or your economic or social level. All that is what you have and what you do, not what you are. You are the Being or Soul and as such you have a name, a body, a job ... You are the Soul "having" a human life.

Part 3: *Atma*

Atma means "soul" in Sanskrit. This third part will lead you to better understand your existence and experience as a soul or being incarnated in a body. Find out what you are made of!

What am I?

You are not your car, but the driver. You are not your body, but the
inhabitant.

When someone asks who you are, you usually answer with your first name, your last name, your profession, your marital status, etc. However, are you really all that?

If instead of your name you had another name, would it change your existence? The answer is no. In fact, before you were named, you already existed. When you're in the subway, bus or plane where nobody knows your name, you don't cease to exist, therefore, you are not your name. Your name is something you have, but it is not what you are.

Your last name refers to the family you belong to, but we've only used last names for a couple thousand years. If you change your last name, or if you don't know your family or if they are no longer here, you will not cease to exist. This means that you are not your last name either, you just have it the same as your name.

In the same way, before studying or having the job you have, you also existed, so again, your degrees, certificates and profession are not what you are but what you do. And when you can no longer practice and you retire, you will not disappear, you will simply be doing something else, perhaps resting.

This happens with every way you want to define yourself; your marital status is not who you are, it's who you are with. Your car, house and money are not what you are, it's what you have or where you are. Even if you go beyond the fear of death and observe just before you were born and just after you die, you will see that you still exist, so you are not even the human being. Your body is the vehicle of the being.

In order to get closer to who you really are, do this little exercise: Start by paying attention to your breathing. Breathe and stay aware that you're breathing, feel the air coming in and out of your lungs. Now take it a step further, not only be aware of the breath, but realize that you are aware that you are aware. Notice that there are two things happening at the same time; first you are conscious; second, you are also aware of the fact that you are aware. You will see that there is the feeling of an observer or someone contemplating. Allow yourself to feel it, with your eyes closed if you want, for a minute repeat in your mind "I am aware that I am aware."

What is that "observer"? That is what you truly are, the soul. This soul is also called in other religions or traditions "I Am", Higher Self, Spirit or Individual Consciousness. You are not a human being that has a soul, you are the soul that is in the body.

When you eat, there is the food, the act of eating and the one who eats. In the same way is your human, the experiences you live and what your soul experiences.

In the process of creation everything was One, all light and consciousness remained in unity until creation happened. Then different parts of that universal light and consciousness became densified and acquired individuality in the form of souls, yet to incarnate physically. Finally, these individual souls observe nature and are attracted to those experiences, which causes them to incarnate in bodies like the one you now have. Your soul is therefore the true essence of who you are.

Each soul is individual and totally complete and autonomous, the idea of soul mates is a false illusion born from people's expectations for a fantasy world in which to evade. God doesn't create a soul and then divide it in two and put one part in one country and the other in another country so that they finally meet. That doesn't make any sense. If there were soul mates, then it would mean that we should always be an even number of each species and die together because if not, half a soul remains out there loose. Moreover, this would imply that we are not autonomous and we would depend on that other soul. The idea of being better halves is romantic but means being incomplete.

You are a whole being and when you are with someone, now there are two whole beings. However, it's true that in each incarnation you are with some souls that you have previously met, not every soul, only a few, and this doesn't mean that you are soulmates or that you have to marry or have sex with them, they are simply acquaintances. You must choose reality versus fantasy, return to simplicity. You are a totally independent and autonomous being and as such, you have the right to enjoy relationships as a couple. Stop looking for your soul mate and accept a man or woman in your life to love, respect and be happy.

As you incarnate, your soul experiences your body in a similar way to how you relate to your car. You have a car, but you know that you are not that car. Every morning you get in it and drive, but you never think you are the car. In the same way, it is your soul that "drives" your body. A part of your soul inhabits and forms your body and the vast majority is around it because it is so large, that it doesn't fit completely inside of you. You can't see it because it's your soul (the observer) that sees it. It's like wanting to see your eye inside, you can't because the eye is what sees. However, if you pay attention to it, as you did in the previous exercise, you can realize that it is there and feel the tranquility it gives.

Your soul is indestructible and eternal, it doesn't die, it cannot become ill or suffer as human beings suffer, because it is made of consciousness and not of matter or emotions. Saying "my soul hurts" is a dramatic way of saying that it hurts a lot, but it's not the soul that is suffering. Even the way your individual consciousness experiences death is completely different from how it is perceived by humans. For the soul, death is nothing but a change of car and instead of living it with mourning and pain, it experiences it with hope and joy just as when you buy a new car, you do not mourn or cry for the old car.

Therefore, if you are the soul, can you even claim that you are alive? No. From the point of view of the human being and nature of course, you are alive, however, from the point of view of the soul, of what you truly are, you are not alive and you are not dead, because again, life It is not what you are but what you do, what you experience as Being. This doesn't mean that then we don't take care of our body, because you take care of your car to last as long as possible. In the same way, you must take care of your body and your life to be and stay as healthy as possible.

You are the soul making your life. You are the indestructible Being.

You can contemplate the following mantra by repeating it for about 20 minutes a day for 12 days in a row. This is called "charging" a mantra and its purpose is to have that energy and awareness in you. Then you can use it whenever you want to connect with your soul.

Aham Nivedin, Aham Atma

Aham in Sanskrit means "I am". *Nivedin* means "to be aware" and *Atma* means soul. Therefore, this mantra means: "I am what is and remains conscious, I am soul."

In your day to day remember: my job is not what I am, it's what I do; my name and last name are not what I am, they are what I use; my body is not what I am, it's what I have; my life is not what I am it's what I experience. I am the Self behind all these experiences.

What is Joy?

Laugh, smile, be happiness.

Joy is a life experience, a state of being and like every experience, it is different for everyone who lives it. However, it has things in common for everyone.

You are not a human being that has a soul, but quite the contrary, a Soul that has a human being. Above the Soul is the Divine part that we all are and that you want to discover. Therefore, in short, you are formed by a Divine part, a part of consciousness or Soul and the Human being.

Each of these parts of you experiences joy in a different way, as each of these parts has a different perception.

For the human being, joy is an explosion of happiness, fun, stimulation and excitement with big laughers, often shared with others. It´s also the happiness of the achieved goals and the satisfaction for the life we have. In this happiness there is a great deal of drama in the exaggeration of the experiences, that is what makes it so vivid. And precisely that intensity makes it a peak very intense and high, but very short in time. The funniest joke can make you cry tears of joy, but 5 minutes later the joke and joy are over, until the next joke.

From the Soul´s point of view, there is simplicity in joy. There is no longer drama because it is not only the acceptance of things as they are, but the enjoyment of any experience without differentiating one as better than another. There is no laughter and guffaws but a state of Joy, which at first seems subtle, but turns out to be much deeper and satisfying. It is a soft smile filled with satisfaction for mere existence. This happiness is independent from the outside because it is born of recognizing ourselves as beings and remain in contact with our consciousness. Metaphorically, it would be something like having a soft smile on your face forever. Because this happiness doesn´t come from outside, but from your essence then it is not limited in time and doesn´t come from the ups and downs that we as human beings experience. There is no explosion as such, but the constant state of being of joy. Like a tea bag infusing itself in hot water, very slowly, but from deep inside becoming intense.

From God's point of view, joy is an experience that we call non-distinction. In divine happiness there is no explosion of joy and fun, but there is also no absence of explosions of joy and fun. There is no simplicity or satisfaction, but there is also no absence of simplicity or satisfaction. Everything is Happiness because Nothing is. It is a completely neutral experience filled by both ends. It is the indefinite (not unconditional) joy of a father contemplating his children. There is no way to understand it with the mind, until one day you experience it, then this answer will seem obvious to you.

How to go from human happiness to that of the soul? How much do you need to be ecstatic, why, what for?

In a previous exercise, you practiced the explosion of laughter through intensely contemplating smiley faces. Now we want to delve into the experience of the soul. To do this, take a moment of the day when you are not in a hurry and sit with your eyes closed. Repeat every 3 to 5 seconds the word "joy" (or in Sanskrit *Sukhi*). No matter what your mind thinks and if it wanders, just focus on repeating: Joy (*Sukhi*) for at least 20 minutes straight. It's like when there's an infusion of tea, you put the tea bag in boiling water and give it time to simmer. In the same way, you allow yourself to be infused gently but deeply into that state of joy, without motives, without explosions. Have no expectations of what or how to feel it, let yourself discover your own way and then stay there in that state for as long as you want.

Life mission

Your life is like a blank book, you write it.

Free will means that you are free to do whatever you want. Life mission means that you have a mission to achieve and therefore you are not free to choose. Therefore, you cannot believe in free will and have a life mission at the same time, because it is contradictory.

If we all have a spiritual life that we must achieve and we all have to become healers or spiritual guides, then... Who is going to prepare the bread that we eat? Who is going to repair the roads? Who is going to design the computer you use?

There is no life mission or purpose to achieve. God did not send you here with a goal to accomplish.

The idea of a "life mission" is born from three misunderstandings:

1) The separation you perceive between spiritual people and non-spiritual people. Where spiritual people are "special" and have a mission / gift that others don't have. It is wanting to be superior. However, all human (and sentient) beings come from the same origin whatever (God / light / consciousness), so we have all been created in the same way. We are all equal, everyone has the ability to develop any gift or ability. No one is more important than others, no one is better than anyone and no one is essential. Every time you see and judge a "non-spiritual" person, remember that you were like that a few years ago or a few lifetimes ago. Have compassion for them. You are not special, nobody is.

2) The need to give meaning to life and existence. When you have a life mission you feel that you have something noble to do, that you have a purpose here, therefore you don't feel so empty or lost. But the solution to this void is not to create a dream or fantasy of something divine to do, but to go into that void and fill it with your own consciousness. Understand it and make yourself self-contained.

3) Your soul. As a human being you have certain features such as the color of your eyes or your hair, as Soul you have an individual and particular point of view. In fact, your soul is a point of view of the whole existence and of God. Having that point of view makes you perceive life and incarnation in a certain way and some seers or healers confuse your point of view with the mission of life. Your point of view is how your Soul perceives, not a job to be done. For example, a soul can perceive transformation through the expansion of compassion. But that is how that soul perceives, not its life mission to be accomplished.

For this reasons many people spend their lives trying to figure out their life's mission, paying psychics to reveal them and often frustrated at not finding it, because they don't like what they found, or disappointed at not fulfilling it, or after doing so, discovering that this was not their mission. Think about it, if it existed and you found it, that means that you can fulfill it and then what? After fulfilling it, you have to die?

A lie repeated a thousand times does not become truth; it remains a lie. To believe and create a life mission is to build an unreal fantasy in which you want to live and it remains a false illusion. You must choose to live in reality, not in the clouds.

You must accept and observe that existential void within you without trying to fill it with justifications but with your own conscience, be self-contained. Then the fear of not knowing stops hurting. Why are we here? What is the meaning of life? The answer is: Here you are. No answer is going to change the fact that you exist. However, existence changes when you embrace it without judgment or questions.

When you finally free yourself from that fantasy, you regain your freedom and instead of asking "what is my life mission?" you will ask yourself "what do I want to do?" And that will be your goal temporarily and the objective to walk towards. You are free, you always have been. Your path is blank as a book, and you write it.

Later on, if you want to discover what the point of view of your soul is, you can do this exercise: Pay attention to your breath and your abdomen, and repeat in your mind or aloud *ParamAtma* which means in Sanskrit "beyond the soul". Meditating on this word will help you feel and understand what your soul's point of view is.

How does the soul perceive?

Seeing, hearing, touching, smelling and feeling are exactly the same.

The human being perceives through the 5 senses: sight, hearing, taste, smell and touch. These senses are active 24 hours a day from birth to death. Have you noticed? At this moment your main active sense is sight because you are reading, but the reality is that if you pay attention you will realize that you are touching the book, you hear the background noise, you are smelling even though there is no specific scent and in your mouth you have the taste of your own saliva or perhaps a recent coffee. Even when you sleep you are awakened by noises or a wrinkle in the sheet and your eyes are looking inside your eyelids, it is only a part of the brain that is disconnected.

If you don't have any disabilities, your senses are always working. There is no way to separate one sense from the others, you can never only see without smelling, hearing, feeling the contact with your clothes or tasting your mouth at the same time. You may not be aware of it, but that doesn't change the fact that your senses are active. Therefore, perception becomes a single event, a single thing happening. Right now, you are not just "seeing" this book, you are smelling, tasting, feeling and hearing it. Just as the pure color is white and as it passes through a glass prism it is divided into the rainbow of infinite colors, "everything" is just an event happening and your senses divide it, like the prism, into five events that are your five senses. But the reality is not these five divisions, but the event happening in unity.

Your soul does not have eyes, ears, mouth, nose or hands; therefore, it cannot divide experiences through the senses. Instead, the soul experiences everything as a single action that is aware of and contemplating. The soul perceives the event happening before the filter of the prism, before the division of the senses, therefore, in a way closer to the Truth, since it is free from human interpretations.

To understand a little more, think of a song that you love, a food that you like a lot, or in your favorite color. You got them? Okay, now try to remember when did you decide that you were going to like each of those things. Do you realize that you can't remember when you decided you were going to like brown or blue? The reason is because you never chose it, it happened.

Your tastes and preferences are not decisions that you have made consciously, but the mix of potentials. If in an environment where everything is positive, you put a potential of something neutral or a little negative, this potential will be stained and become positive and vice versa. For example, remember as a child a day at school when you failed an exam and the teacher scolded you and sent you to have your parents sign the exam. When you got home, your teenage brother pushed you, the neighbor's dog that you were afraid of was barking and on that day your mother was angry at your father. Now, in that negative environment they gave you fish for the first time ... and since then you have not liked fish or vegetables.

On another occasion, there was a song that you didn't like at all, but one day you were trying to conquer your crush, enjoying the company and the evening, you were feeling love and at that moment that song you didn't like, started to play and the person you were in love with started singing it while smiling at you ... and since then you love that song even if you're not with that person anymore. Do you remember?

In both situations it was not a conscious decision, it was not a matter of the taste of fish or of musical preferences, but a combination of all the potentials happening at that time without distinction of senses. In these events, your soul observed the situation in a global perspective and declared "I don't like fish", "I like that song" and so it happens every day with every event you live. For your soul to see, hear, smell, taste and touch, it´s a unique experience, it´s all the same without distinction.

Indraikya means all the senses are *one*. Meditate for long periods of time (minimum 25 minutes) on this mantra to turn this theory into practice, then you will begin to perceive how your soul perceives.

If the soul is being conscious, perception is the contemplation and awareness of the event happening as a Whole, in unity and knowing that the experiences are neither good nor bad but only events happening, potentials mixing.

Passion

In the universe everything loves everything. Be the universe.

"I am in love" with no one or anything in specific as the object of that love and without excluding anything or anyone from it.

There is more love and passion than hate and suffering in life. There are more people who help you get up if you fall on the street than those who would ignore you. There are many more displays of love than of resentment. More mothers and fathers taking care of their children than abandoned children. More lovers showing their affection, people passionate about their jobs, dogs taking care of cats. People who smile at you, greet you and say "*bon appetite*" when eating. You don't need to be personally and egocentrically involved to see and feel that love, for it is there, and being aware of it makes you feel as if you were involved in every love event.

Just 75 years ago almost the entire planet was at war (World War II), today only 5-8% of the planet remains at war, in the rest there are no more international conflicts. Only 15 or 20 years ago, women were tremendously discriminated, without the right to vote or to a decent job. Today we all have the same rights and the rate of gender abuse has decreased dramatically in most countries. 5 or 10 years ago homosexuals were discriminated, imprisoned, beaten and even killed in most parts of the planet. Today there are more and more states and countries that allow marriage and adoption, providing exactly the same rights to everyone regardless of their sexuality. Hunger in the world has decreased and safety on the streets is much better than before.

When you are stuck in traffic, before feeling angry, look at the cars around you and be aware that one of them is going to work so that you have internet at home, another is going to clean the floor of the shopping center where you shop, someone is going to manufacture the furniture you use, another takes the food to your supermarket, etc.

If you objectively look at the total of your life, you have always gotten ahead of even the worst situations and there was almost always someone willing to help, maybe not like you wanted them to, yet someone has helped you in your life and you got over it.

This doesn't mean that today's humanity and society is perfect, to affirm that, would be an extreme optimist. As a society, we still have many steps to take, many things to improve and we must work together and strive to achieve it, but the objective evidence shows that we are doing well, that we are actually doing very well. We are evolving and each day we take a further step towards awareness and compassion.

Open your eyes and see the great team we all are, collaborating like pieces of a puzzle where each piece is important and fundamental. Discover the passion of some people taking care of others and vice versa. And now include yourself, since you are also a piece of this great puzzle. Every day someone is benefiting from your work, whatever it may be, so you are also collaborating with the improvement and evolution of humanity. Contemplate it and allow your passion for wanting to collaborate with everyone to explode inside you, an internal infiltration of beauty and love for this life and society in which we are.

There is love and passion, that's why I love.

Karma

Karma are the actions that take care of you.

Each experience you live and each event that happens to you is generated by three possible options:

• *Dharma*: These are experiences originated from the soul with the purpose of learning and understanding a certain situation. Metaphorically, they are the desires and curiosities of your soul. Just like sometimes you feel like going to the movies, your soul wants certain experiences so it manifests them in your life.

• *Karma*: They are the consequences of your previous actions, it is neither good nor bad, nor is it a punishment or blessing. It's just the result; it's the cause and effect of your actions.

• *Prikti*: These are the events that happen because we are in nature. They have no further explanation or meaning, they happen simply by being incarnated. There are laws of nature and they affect us. They have no symbolism. They are generally smooth and pass very quickly. They are only 5% of what we live.

With time and experience, you can differentiate when something happens to you by *dharma, karma* or *prikti,* just as with training you can differentiate a good wine from a bad one. In terms of problem solving, it doesn't matter what the source of your discomfort is because the solution is the same in all three cases: Observe, accept and feel the discomfort to dissolve. Knowing this distinction helps you understand that not everything is karmic, although most events are. So, what is karma?

In the Spanish or English alphabet, the letters have no meaning. The "B" or "G" don't mean anything. However, in Sanskrit and Hebrew each letter has a meaning. For example, the letter "B" means to contain and the "G" means to expand. These meanings are based on the language of the soul, which are the universal sounds that we naturally make. For example, when you are looking for something and suddenly you find it, you spontaneously say "Ah, there it is"; in Sanskrit and Hebrew the "A" means presence. When something hurts, you usually exclaim "Uuuu" and the "U" means what you feel or experience. When something is immense or beautiful and it surprises you, like fireworks, you say "Ohhhhh" and the "O" means immensity and so on with each vowel or consonant. This is how Sanskrit mantras (power phrases) are formed and that is why they are so efficient, because they speak the universal language of consciousness.

Following this explanation, the word Karma has a letter-by-letter meaning. The "K" means Cause or provoke; the "A" presence; the "R" means to define or intense. So, the syllable "Kar" means to cause in an intense and present way, to provoke an action; the "M" is the letter of the ocean, the consciousness or energy, and "Ma" then means in the consciousness or energy of a present form. Therefore, Karma means to provoke a present action in your energy. As you see, here there is no reference to punishment, evil or suffering because it simply is not. Not only it's not bad, but another meaning of the syllable "Ma" refers to the feminine energy of caring and protecting, so we could add that Karma is the present actions that take care of you. And this is much more accurate with Truth. Your karma takes care of you.

There is no good or bad in life, there are only perceptions based on belief systems, social or religious. What may be good for one person, may be bad for another and vice versa. However, there is something common in all our actions and in which we can all agree beyond belief. There are 3 types of actions: 1) actions that promote joy; 2) neutral actions that generate nothing; 3) actions that cause suffering. Now you can set aside the good and the bad and observe the actions from this new perspective that is much more universal than the good and the bad.

Every day, each of your actions produces one of the previous results: joy, neutrality or suffering in you and in your environment. Those actions impact people and nature and bounce back towards you. What comes back to you many times is not exactly the same experience that you generated but the result of your actions, what comes back is the same amount of suffering or joy that you caused. For example, if you break a friend's favorite vase and they suffer, your karma is not necessarily someone breaking a vase of yours, your karma is the suffering your friend experienced. That is what you will get back, if you don't care about vases then nobody will break a vase of yours, because you wouldn't experience the same discomfort that you caused, instead someone may step on your phone and break the screen or you're car's rear mirror, or something that you appreciate as much as your friend appreciated the vase.

In the same way, if you help someone and that person feels very happy, your karma is not that person doing something for you so that you feel happy, maybe someone (that person or another) will want to help you so that you experience the same joy that you caused.

Karma is the result of your actions; it happens literally only sometimes, so you remember and understand your actions because the same experience is going to affect you too. Some simple examples of karma are: you eat a lot of chocolate and gain weight; you diet or exercise, you lose weight; you go to work every day, and at the end of the month you get your paycheck; you miss a day at work, they discount it; you are a very good worker and your bosses are happy with you, and you miss a day at work, then your bosses decide not to discount it; you knock with your hand on a door, karma is the noise emitted and the sensation in your hand. In the same way, if you lie or cheat on someone, your karma is that someone will lie to you and cheat on you so you know what it feels like.

The reason why you are afraid of karma is because you believe that it's only negative and because you know that you have sometimes caused pain to others, you believe that your accumulated karma will be terrible. But do you really think you've done so much damage? Probably not ... and if the answer is yes, take a deep breath, arm yourself with courage, and agree to pay your bills and consequences.

If nothing is going well in your life and everything is suffering, you should consider starting to change your way of acting, thinking and being, to counteract your karma and start generating a new one that causes joy and not suffering.

Remember that every mistake you have made is just a learning step. Don't be hard on yourself, but accept your karma whatever it is.

All your karma is, metaphorically, stored in "your karma account" which we call the plane of karma, causality or experience. There part of the karma of suffering is balanced only with the karma of joy at the consciousness level and doesn't manifest. But sometimes that karma can only be compensated through experiences. Then that kind of karma accumulates until it is so dense that it collapses, falls and now as a human you live that experience. That is why you can have the karma of making money and losing it at the same time. The first as a result of your work and the second as a result of your abuse.

For example, if you manipulate a person to be with you, in your karmic account you put manipulation potentials against you. Later on you manipulate again adding more manipulation potentials and so on until the time comes that all those manipulation potentials are so large that they collapse and it happens that you are left by your partner, nobody wants to be with you and the few who find you interesting all they do is manipulate you over and over again. And here's the other problem, instead of agreeing to pay your karma, you complain and run away, actually creating interests in your account for not wanting to pay it off when the time came. It's not a punishment; it's only the result of your previous actions so that you can understand what you have done to others and thus stop manipulating in the future.

If on the contrary, instead of wanting to be the center of attention and wanting to get all the love for yourself, you start to pay attention to others, to selflessly give love so that they feel happy and loved, then you are putting on your account love karma in your favor. After some time of doing it, it will collapse and in your daily life you will have a lot of friends and people who love you and want to be with you. All because instead of just wanting to receive the love of others, you make them feel loved. Everyone wants to be loved, but someone has to give that love. Be the one who initiates the love movement.

Your karma collapses little by little if you don't do spirituality, or faster when you do, because you agree to pay it off. If at the time of your death there was a pending account then the karma accumulates and will manifest in the next life that your soul experiences. This is because when you die, what dies is only the human part (the last 4 planes of your existence (body, vital plane, emotional and mental) but death does not affect your soul at all. Your karma is accumulated in the soul, in what is known as plane 5 of causality, that is why it is inherited from one life to another. So, it's true that you have karma from past lives, that is a fact. However, the idea that you have to do past life regressions to solve your problems is a misunderstanding.

If in this life you have financial problems, may be part of it is due to the fact that in another life you stole or were greedy. However, realize and observe that the one who is suffering from money problems is you, here and now. You cannot believe in the here and now and at the same time wanting to go back to a past life to solve a problem, because the past does not exist. Your problems are not the human being that existed 200 years ago, that person doesn't exist anymore, is dead. As if in a past life you were a cow, now you are no longer one, nor are you that human being. You have problems and it is only you who must solve them. Do not blame your karma or your past lives for your problems, that's not responsible. It's not necessary to do past life regressions. No matter what the origin of any of your problems is, the solution is always the same: accept to pay your karma and if you do it consciously, then if it's negative, it will be faster and less painful, or more pleasant if it's positive. You have the power to dissolve all your karma here and now, you just need to learn how to do it with awareness.

There are many techniques to resolve and pay for your karma, but they all have one thing in common: you have to feel it, embrace it, and stay aware of it no matter how much it hurts. In fact, the more aware you are of it, the less it will hurt. The fastest and most efficient technique I know of is called Emotional Integration. It was created by the Buddhist Master MahaVajra. It is based on the fact that consciousness is the solvent of any suffering. Therefore, you must put your consciousness into your discomfort. What is this consciousness? Is to pay full attention to what you are feeling, without drama, and breathing at the same time. To be aware is to contemplate something with a true desire to understand it, no matter how dense it is. How does being conscious end your pain? Because any suffering you have is born out of misinterpretation, misunderstanding or judgment and mindfulness brings clarity and understanding to the problem.

In summary, remember that your karma takes care of you, it teaches you to support actions that cause joy and avoid those that cause suffering. Your karma allows everything to balance so that you can evolve and have a life of joy, virtue and love.

If you want to find out more about your karma, you can meditate on the archangel *Tzadkiel*, is the archangel of Divine Justice, is the one who makes sure that everything is balanced. Meditate repeating the name every few seconds for 20 minutes a day for 10 consecutive days. This will help you understand your karma, accept it and collapse as quickly as possible, both the karma of suffering and that of joy.

The 10 Planes of Existence

I am a conscious point of view in the Universe.

Some traditions explain that the human being is formed of four planes, others of five, others of seven, etc. And then, they come into conflict and fight to be right. These differences are due to what each tradition perceives and contemplates. For example, if they ask you about the colors of the rainbow, you would answer the 7 colors that you know, but the reality is that the rainbow has all the existing colors in the spectrum of light and these colors are not separated by a clear line, but they flow and they change smoothly. Therefore, the rainbow has as many colors as labels you want to put on.

It happens like this with our existence; we are not formed of 4, 5, 7 or 10 separate planes or bodies. We are a single stream of consciousness that, like the rainbow, varies in some qualities and, where those characteristics are obvious, we can label them for a better understanding. So, like the rainbow, it can have the amount of colors that you choose to name. The same happens with the human being, we have as many plains as you decide to emphasize.

Understanding that we are a single stream of consciousness or energy, using a classification system will help you to better understand your existence. The best known and accepted throughout history is the division into ten planes or bodies.

It begins by observing that you exist, that the world is real, therefore there is creation. If there is creation then there must be an origin of that creation. For example, if you have a salad in your refrigerator, someone had to make it. Likewise, not someone but "something" produced creation. It's what we call the Creator, Origin or God (not a person). Furthermore, to make that salad, someone had to interact with each ingredient by washing, cutting, and mix it. So that Origin also had an interaction with the creation to be able to do it. It´s what we call the Interaction or Divine Action.

These are the first three planes of existence that form the first category of the Divine Planes:

1) Origin or God. The beginning, the producing principle of Everything.
2) Creation. It is the result of the action of the creator, existence, the universe.
3) Interaction. The relationship and action between Origin and Creation.

These three planes correspond with the Holy Trinity in all religions. Father, Son and Holy Spirit for Christians; *Eheieh, Iah* and *Iaveh* for Kabbalists and Jews; *Brahma, Vishnu* and *Shiva* for the Hindus; *Amitabha, Mahastanaprapta, Avalokiteshwara* for Buddhists; energy, matter and speed for science. The truth is one and each person or religion perceives it from a different point of view. In Spanish we say *"agua"*, water in English, *acqua* in Italian and *apsa* in Sanskrit, but the substance is exactly the same. When religions fight each other, they are fighting for the name to use, but the Truth is the same in all.

Once this consciousness appeared, it began to densify more and more, until through that density, it fell from these first planes, separating and individualizing. Your soul has just appeared, as an individual consciousness package made from that original universal consciousness. Independent and autonomous from other souls.

Now that individual consciousness is like a child who wishes to live experiences, act imitating the creator, and that is how the plane of Causality, also known as the plane of Experiences or the plane of Karma, is born. And each of the experiences that the soul lives, leads to a certain wisdom, thus forming the plane of Wisdom.

These are the Planes of the Soul:

4) Individual consciousness. Just like you can pay attention, your soul can too. You are conscious and your soul is conscious. So, it is your awareness of being aware.

5) Causality or Karma. What that individual consciousness does and generates. The actions. Your karma.

6) Wisdom. The understanding and wisdom obtained through those experiences. Knowledge is knowing that fire burns, wisdom is not touching it.

These 3 planes together form what we call Soul, which is also known as the Higher Self, I Am, the essence or the spirit. All of these are synonymous with your individuality as consciousness.

So far, your physical body does not exist, nor your emotions or thoughts, there is no tangible matter yet. It is just from here that your soul continues to densify, but this densification now reaches a boundary point where it cannot go any further. So, it not only densifies, but it condenses to such an extent that that consciousness is so, so dense that it becomes tangible. Matter, nature and your physical body have just been born as a result of the densification, compression and compaction of your soul.

The mind is formed in this last process, made of thoughts and creativity to produce the rest of nature. The mind is followed by the emotional plane which is the engine or machinery that moves you. If you realize, a thought is much lighter than an emotion, changing your mind is easy, changing an emotion is much more difficult because it is ten times denser. Then these emotions are densified 10% more and the vital plane appears, which is just the energy of your body. If you pay attention and put your empty hands closer as if you were holding a small ball, after about 15 seconds you will feel an energy ball between them. If you try to separate them slowly, you will feel a force pulling your hands together. That is your life plane. Likewise, if you pass your right hand very slowly over your left arm without touching it, about 8-10 cm away, you will see that the sensation feeling of your left arm is like a caress. In fact, in doing so you are caressing your vital plane, that's why it feels nice. This energy plane has the same shape as your physical body and protrudes 8 to 15 cm around. The more meditation you practice, the bigger your vital plane. The function of this plane is to regulate your vital energy.

Finally, the physical body appears as such. It is the final result of the densification process, as when you make a tower of cups and the last ones below are the ones that receive the most wine and are completely filled. Your body is like the last cup that receives all that awareness. It's the densest plane there is. It's 100 times denser than your emotions and 1000 times more than your mind. Hence it's so difficult to change something physically, it is not impossible, it simply requires a lot more work.

Finally, your Planes of Nature or of the Human Being:
7) Mental Plane
8) Emotional Plane
9) Vital Plane
10) Body or physical plane

It is through these last 4 planes that the soul can live the experiences and that the origin of plane 1 can be incarnated.

Each of your 10 planes is a point of view of the whole. Understanding these ten planes of your existence helps you, first to understand yourself and then to understand how creation and consciousness function and flow.

The best way to learn about all these planes is through self-contemplation. To do this, start with the planes of the human being, since they are more dense and easier to perceive. Sit down and pay attention only to your physical body, feel the contact with the chair or floor, be aware of how it feels. You will realize that the first sensation you get is calm and peace. You are becoming aware of your body. Once this step is done, go ahead and try to observe and become aware of the energy of your body, then of your emotions, mind and so on. It's not necessary to have a 100% understanding of each plane, just breathe and contemplate the name of that plane in your mind and in a few minutes, you will begin to perceive it. Be patient, because planes 1 to 6 are so subtle that feeling them takes practice and time, but you will achieve it.

Connect with you

Breathe, inhabit, feel, observe

The five senses are the tools with which we perceive ourselves as humans. They allow us to identify what we need to survive, what is good, and what can be dangerous. But if you notice, they are all focused exclusively outward. You can't see your body inside; you can't touch your internal organs or smell your inside. This is why whenever you need something naturally, you will look for it on the outside, because it is where your senses tell you that it is "everything".

Imagine the conscience that you are like the water contained in a large pool. It has 5 exits, which are the 5 senses, through these exits your consciousness goes outwards allowing you to relate to the world and live. Now imagine what would happen if you open the 5 exits to that pool at the maximum 24 hours a day; it is obvious that the pool would empty quickly.

This is what happens when you invest all your consciousness on the outside, on materialism and wanting to fill yourself from the outside. Every time you look for and need something from the outside to fill your gaps, you are emptying yourself more because your consciousness is moving towards that goal. So, when apparently you have everything in life, sometimes you feel that you are missing something, you feel lonely and you don't understand why. Then the mind sets new challenges such as changing jobs, city, partner, but these are all temporary remedies. What happened is that you emptied your pool and instead of creating new consciousness to fill it again, you try to fill it with the outside, but what you are doing is emptying it more and staying at "negative numbers".

If, on the contrary, you decide to close those 5 exits so that you don't empty yourself, through rejecting the material world, the society and materialism, then you will find that if you put water in a container without movement or oxygenation, it rots, making you feel equally bad.

What is the solution? As always, the middle way, never the ends. Allowing part of your consciousness to come out, accepting and enjoying the material world, society, the people we live with, and at the same time constantly filling your pool with new consciousness through meditation and spirituality. The best balance you can achieve is when you always have a little more conscience on the inside than on the outside. This is a good middle ground where you will never feel empty.

How to know how you are at this moment? Pay attention inside of you, and let yourself feel on the margins of your material achievements, on the margins of your life…. Do you feel empty or lonely? Are you unsatisfied? If so, then you need to fill yourself up a little more so that abandonment disappears.

This is called being self-contained, it means containing yourself. To achieve this, practice the following exercise daily for 5 to 15 minutes and you will see how those feelings of loneliness and need diminish, and your personal satisfaction increases.

It is known as "Meditation of the 4 states" and it consists of these 4 steps:

1) Breathe. This is a mindful breathing in which you breathe from your abdomen. Breathing in instead of inflating your lungs, allow your abdomen to come out, and breathing out your abdomen comes in. So much more oxygen enters your lungs. Now do it but also be aware that you are breathing. Feel the air entering your lungs, traveling through your body, and coming out again. After a few inhalations add the state of "I am aware that I am aware" in your mind. This first step helps you relax and get in touch with yourself.

2) Inhabit. Now you will try to inhabit your body. For this, imagine that your body is the pajamas of your soul, imagine your soul dressing with your body. Imagine how your soul dresses with your legs, your hips, your back, your chest, your arms and finally your head. This is to inhabit and exist in your body, to incarnate. Put your intention and willpower and

you will feel that consciousness entering your body. This second step allows you to embody yourself. Incarnation is how your consciousness and soul enter your body and make you healthier, concentrate better, and live more intensely.

3) Feel. Once your consciousness is back inside you (in your pool) it is time to let yourself feel. Pay attention to how it feels to be in the body and aware. It is to enjoy the pleasant bath in that pool. Don't pay attention or get hooked on any particular emotion, just let yourself feel. This third step helps you connect with your emotions and fill in your emotional voids with your conscience.

4) Observe. Finally, we engage the mind. If in the previous step you felt the sensations, now you have to observe without judgment, without ideas, just contemplate the entire experience. Without any particular thought, nor denying the thoughts. It's as if you were in a viewpoint at the top of a mountain and from there you observe the landscape and the entire city. This last step calms your mind and fills the mental voids and uncertainties with your consciousness, it helps you understand and be objective.

"Breathe, inhabit, feel, observe" is the meditation that you do by repeating each of these states cyclically for a few seconds as mantras, until all 4 become a single state: being conscious.

With these 4 states you will be able to generate new and pure consciousness again, to fill back your pool, feel good and now allow part of your conscience to flow out again.

Compassion

Even the deepest pain is a temporary learning experience.

A Virtue is a noble, pure behavior based on awareness and the desire to promote joy and well-being. A vice is a behavior that hurts and harms us or others. There are many virtues such as peace, forgiveness, gratitude, prudence, justice, etc. Buddha claimed that Compassion is the most difficult and the most important to develop.

We cannot define compassion in words, because they are attitudes, behaviors and actions that vary according to the situation. Therefore, you have to look at it from different points of view.

First of all, don't confuse mercy or pity with compassion. The origin of pity is comparison. Every time you feel sorry or pity for someone, what happens is you're comparing yourself to that person and you win. When you lose, now you think you deserve that pity. Of course, it doesn't seem like that at first, so you need to look more deeply. When you say "Oh, poor man who has no place to sleep" it's what you say, but in your mind the phrase continues like this: "... and I do." "Poor thing who has nothing to eat" and in your mind "... and I do." "Poor handicapped man who can't walk ... and I can." Do you realize that? Have you ever felt bad or sorry for a rich billionaire? Most likely your answer is "yes, because everyone loves them only for their money" and in your mind "... and I am loved for who I am" and just found something in which you are better than billionaires to be able to pity them.

This attitude helps absolutely no one, in fact, it only makes things worse and creates more suffering. Remember when perhaps one day you got sick and your family and friends felt sorry for you, treating you as if you were inferior, you didn't like it at all. Well, that's what other people feel when you feel sorry for them. By doing so, you look down on them because unconsciously you are affirming that they don't have the ability or the means to solve their problem, which is not true.

Compassion is understanding that there is no good or bad and that what we go through are experiences that give us the opportunity to learn and evolve through them. Compassion is to stop seeing suffering where it appears to be and instead, see the hidden experience behind what you and others live. With compassion, the drama disappears and the suffering gradually dissolves because only the Truth can prevail.

Compassion is the fourth noble truth of Buddhism: "There is no suffering." But in order to experience it, you cannot deny what you are experiencing and try to convince yourself that it's not real, when everything shows you that it apparently is. To be able to feel that there is no suffering, you must go through the first 3 noble truths: 1) there is suffering; 2) your suffering has an origin, find it; 3) observe and stay aware of that origin, so you will be traveling the path of liberation from suffering; 4) once you have traveled all the way now you will discover that there is no suffering.

When you feel bad and you are in drama, this is the way to go. When you finish it and realize that in that subject there is no longer suffering, you gain the ability to see someone in that same situation and know that there is no suffering in the end, that they should walk through the same path you did. This doesn't mean saying to the people "Hey, there is no suffering" because they will not understand you or they will use your words to deny the problem. Instead, you must observe them from the firmness that there is no suffering, but at the same time understand that they are convinced that there is, and understand that they must recognize the 3 previous noble truths.

It's from there that you can apply compassion and help them with their pain, not save them because then they wouldn't learn the lesson and manifest it again later, but help is always good and welcome.

This is the complexity of the virtue of compassion, because you can only remain compassionate on those issues and situations that you have already resolved in yourself. You cannot have compassion for a liar if you judge or are bothered by lies. Your fear of poverty keeps you from feeling compassion, rather than pity for the poor. You can't have compassion for someone who's sick if you are afraid of disease. On every topic you haven't worked on yet, you haven't gone through the 4 steps either. Therefore, you still see suffering in those experiences and naturally pity and fear will be activated within you, instead of compassion.

Don't judge your current level of compassion, that wouldn't be compassionate to yourself. The reality is that in many aspects of your life you are able to remain in compassion, and in the rest, you are gradually taking a step further.

Some practical examples will help you understand better:

-If your son or daughter throws you a tantrum at the mall and you pay attention, then they are going to do it every time they want something and they are going to be constantly manipulating you. However, what most mothers do is tell their kids "let me know when you are done crying and we'll talk" and they turn around so that their children understand that this is not the way. In the same way, adults and you, have these tantrums and as a compassionate person, the best thing you can do to help is to observe with the awareness that there is no suffering and from there, make the necessary decision so that they can grow and travel their path and learn.

-Before a person emotionally dependent on others, who always seeks the appreciation and approval of others, giving them constant signs of love and affection increases their dependence. This is not compassionate. In this case, the most compassionate thing that can be done is that, when this person is activated by the addiction for attention, deny it so they can see their lack and inner emptiness.

-A spiritual teacher used to finish all his courses hugging all the participants because he liked to close with love and compassion. However, if you have that rule, how are you going to know when someone doesn't like you and is wanting you to finish and leave? How are you going to know if among the attendees there is a woman who has experienced sexual abuse and by hugging her you are actually activating that memory right at the end of the course? Compassion is not a rule, but to remain in consciousness, then you will see how consciousness and energy flow and what step or movement is the best for everyone.

Compassion is when a mother or father make their children eat healthy for their well-being. Or have them infinite patience to handle their reproaches and complaints while they're in their teens because they remember that they too were teenagers.

It is giving a coin or doing charity by helping someone who needs it, not out of pity but out of an understanding of the experience that person is going through, knowing that they will solve it and you are just making it easier for them.

It's smiling at someone on the street who's sad, so they know there is also joy in life. It's giving a hug to the one who is going to be helped by it and denying it to the one who is going to become addicted.

Compassion sometimes seems to go against good manners or social rules. These happens because in fact, most people are not compassionate, so all these rules establish a pattern of behavior to decrease suffering in society, but there comes a point where they fall short and you have to develop compassion beyond education, as it is much deeper and beneficial for all.

In order to act from compassion, realize the pure understanding of the situation you face, to discover that there is no suffering either and from there, observe, help others and yourself so that you can walk the path of liberation from suffering. Then you will know how to act at all times.

Do what you have to do for the benefit of all, sometimes it will be tender, loving and sweet, but sometimes it will be severe, direct and confrontational. Act from consciousness and love, not from insecurity, fear or pity and you will be a compassionate being.

You can help yourself with the Mantra of Compassion *Om mani padme hum*, reciting it repeatedly for 20 minutes 12 days in a row. This meditation will help you to stop believing in drama, yours and others, as well as to achieve greater awareness and understanding of each situation you live.

Interlude 3: God is the answer

God is the answer:
No matter what your question is
God is the answer.

No matter how much you suffer
God is the answer.

It doesn't matter if you don't understand
If you don't feel it, if you don't live it
If you don't see it, if you don't hear it
God is the answer.

It doesn't matter if you know or are aware
It doesn't even matter if you agree
God is still the answer.

Observe all your questions with a firm mind that God is the answer until
so.
Then you will open your eyes, wake up, and there will be no more
questions. You will only see God around you.
Then you will look at a mirror and see in it the answer: God

God is the answer

Be all blessed

Part 4: Brahma

Brahma in Sanskrit defines how we unite the concepts of the Holy Trinity and all aspects related to the divine. In this fourth part you will study and learn about the highest planes of your being and existence.

What is God?

If your God exists, it is not the true one. If your God does not exist, it is the good one.

Does God exist? What is God? These are some of the most common questions people ask. Each religion has its own definition -which often leads to more confusion- and these definitions have even led to conflict and war. God is not something that we can fit into a definition because God is precisely the definitor and it's not possible to define the definitor.

If you consider that God is a man with a white beard, then who created that man? Likewise, if God is white light, where did that light come from? In the Bible, Genesis 1: 3 says "... And God said there is light and there was light..." This verse shows you that God is not the light but the one who made it and that before there was light God already existed. When in the Bible it says "God said" it's not literal, since God has no mouth like a person, it's a metaphor. To think God is a person (man or woman) is tremendously arrogant and self-centered because there are many other life forms such as animals, insects, plants, planets, stars, etc., that have the same origin as us.

In order to live the experience of God, you must let go of all the judgments and definitions that you have up to this moment.

Remember all the negative things that you think, have been taught, or have heard about God, all that anger, rage, reproaches ... and let them go, because that is not God. Now remember all the positive about God and let that go too, because that is not God either, those are just more definitions. If you are convinced that God doesn't exist, you have no proof of it, so let this idea go as well. If you're convinced that God does exist, you don't have proof either, so let it go too. Empty yourself completely. If a glass is full you cannot fill it. If you are full of definitions, how can you discover your Truth?

After emptying yourself of your definitions of God, if you pay attention inside, you will see that now there is a feeling of uncertainty, insecurity and perhaps fear. This exercise causes some people to panic. Just as you once invented a false plan to survive financially out of fear, you do exactly the same with God. Panic and insecurity push you to create a definition and fantasy of God just to calm that fear. But this definition is not real, it is based on illusions, fantasies, other people's beliefs and opinions, not on your own experience.

Buddha was approached by a disciple and asked, "Master, does Brahma exist?" (as they call God in Hinduism) to which Buddha replied: "of course not." Later a second disciple approached him and asked, "Master, does Brahma exist?" and Buddha replied, "of course Brahma exists." A third disciple approaches him and asks the same question, to which Buddha replies: "Neither exists, nor lacks of existence." In all 3 cases Buddha was telling the Truth, the answer to these 3 disciples is the same and it is true in all cases.

The first student had a definition of God as a human being with 4 arms and several heads, as they draw and represent in Hinduism, a god you must pray to save you without you doing anything but pray and that is not real. Therefore, the God this student contemplated does not exist. The second disciple, however, did not have these definitions, but wanted to know about the origin of creation and know that we can come to understand and experience God, so the Buddha clearly answered that there is a beginning or origin to give him a motivation to continue. Finally, the third disciple was the most advanced of all, and so Buddha explained to him the middle way, where you cannot cling to the definition or existence of God, nor can you cling to the non-existence or lack of God.

To the question what is God? what you really need is to dissolve the question, not to repress or deny it, but to go inside to that place full of anguish, insecurity and fear, and instead of trying to hide it and fill it with false ideas, stay there, in the " non-definition ". Stay conscious of the uncertainty and fear, until you have adapted and get used to it and the need for the answer will be gone. Then you will have freed yourself from the judgments and you will be able to discover your own experience of what God is.

Begin by contemplating "God is all." But to affirm that "God is all" is a definition because God is also "nothing." To affirm "God is love" is also a definition. So, remove those definitions and contemplate "God is." Breathe and let yourself feel this.

But again, this is a definition because "God is also not." Then remove the "is" and contemplate only: "God." Breathe again, feel and you will see that there is a sense of Truth purer than before.

Now take one more step, "God" is also a definition, so take it out too, now immerse yourself and fill yourself with the true experience without definition.

Contemplate: ""

That is your truth.

Conquer your attachments

Thanks to attachments love can flow.

An attachment is the bond you create with material things, with people, and with your own identity. It's like a chain that links the object of attachment to you and through which the relationship, energy, love or hate flows. Some philosophies say that you must live free of material attachments and without emotional ties. The only way to do this is to isolate yourself in nature without having contact with anyone or anything, this is not a life free of attachments, but of repression. If you consider the creation of the world to be perfect and that people and material things exist, then they must be so that we can enjoy and experience them. God made no mistake in creating relationships, material things, or our identity.

Attachments are not bad, on the contrary, it is thanks to attachments that parents take care, protect and give love to their children; attachment to our identity makes us evolve and want to be better; attachment to material things gives us the possibility of living a life of comfort and physical stability.

The human mind is accustomed to thinking of duality exclusively, on the extremes. We define things as black or white, yes or no, therefore it is tremendously difficult to understand the middle path as the place of balance. Your mind knows what it is to have something (+1) and also knows what it is to lack something (-1) but then what is "0"? What is it not to have something, but also not to lack something? That is the experience of the middle path and balance, the mind can't understand it because it is not logical, it's an experience. Because of this, you spend a large part of your time hovering from +1 to -1, that is, from one end to the other, until one day you get tired and decide to come to rest and stop at 0, then you will have discovered the middle path.

Due to this duality, before being spiritual everyone is materialistic who reject the divine and spiritual world, because only the material and relationships matter. They are at +1 in reference to attachments. Then they suffer from this dependence on the outside and begin their spiritual path, they see how much energy and consciousness they have wasted on material and emotional attachments and then they reject the material, mundane world because it is "not spiritual" and wish to live a life free of attachments. Now they are in -1 and likewise suffer from the repression of attachments and desires.

Now that you know these two ends, you are ready to take the final step, to find the middle point. To do this, you have to accept that of course, every time you have attachments, part of your consciousness and energy goes through them. It's true that every time you become attached, you start looking outside for joy, love and peace, and that everything you get from the outside is ephemeral, later on you will have to find it inside. But getting joy, love or peace from the outside is not a bad thing, it is how we have been created. If you believe that God is Everything and Everywhere then God is also a relationship, a car, a phone, an orgasm or social networks.

Don't be afraid of "losing consciousness" by enjoying the "worldly" life. Consciousness is like money, if you don't move and invest it, you lose it. If you don't allow the flow of consciousness through attachments, your consciousness "rots." Learn to produce new consciousness through your meditation and spirituality instead, so you always have resources to share and use.

Accept to be attached to everyone and to all the experiences in your life that bring you joy or love in any way, allow the flow of consciousness. Embrace worldly and material life at the same time. And learn to let go and come back to yourself.

The problem is not the attachments, but your pride, shame and fear that keep you from letting go and release when the time comes. What hurts you is wanting to nail what's already ended, sometimes out of dependence, sometimes out of fear of failure.

Nothing is eternal, everything that has a beginning, has an end and this end is not a failure, but the natural and normal process of life. For example, someone who dies didn't fail to be alive, they died because it is the law of life and it'll happen to all of us. In the same way, when you lose your job, your relationship or a good friend, it is not a failure, it's the natural end of all cycles. Don't be hard on yourself, accept that one day it would end and when that day comes, release and let go.

There are 3 types of attachments, the first is the Material, Physical or Possessions attachment: it's the attachment to your things and material objects such as your car, your house, your watch, your phone, your clothes, your money, etc. It has power over you because you are convinced that these are "yours", but in reality, they aren't. It is not "your" house, it is the house where you live. It is not "your" car, it is a car that you use. You were born with nothing and when you die you will go with nothing.

To conquer your attachments is to let go when the time comes. Don't allow them to have power over you, but you remain with mastery over them. An example of conquest of material attachment is the following, it happened to me some time ago:

On a Monday I got my brand-new car, on Friday a clueless bus hits me, breaking the rear bumper of the new car. When the driver, a boy about 17 years old, got out he started yelling at me as if it were my responsibility. It turned out that the bus didn't have insurance so probably it was going to be necessary to go to trial or reach an economic settlement right there. At that moment the owner of the bus, who has just arrived, tells the driver "it was your fault and you'll see if you get a deal, if he takes you to court, it will be more expensive because you are going to pay for it, then you manage." The driver comes back holding a $200 MXN bill (about 15 USD) that he took out from the ATM and in the other hand, $200 MXN in coins, that is all his friends could lend him, totally ashamed and in humility accepting his responsibility. At that moment in front of all the people who had come to see, I said: "This boy has done nothing wrong, it was just an accident and it's not fair that you

145

(talking to the owner of the bus) leave him with the problem when you have no insurance and hold him accountable. Accidents happen and you must protect your workers. "

Then, turning to the driver, I said: "if you give me that $400 MXN ($30 USD), you will get into debt because you don't have that money and you won't be able to pay your bills, so that's not fair, you haven't done anything wrong. Instead, how much can you give me without seriously affecting your economy?" I asked. "$50 MXN" about ($3 USD), answered the teenage driver, so that was the amount I accepted because it was the fairest. This boy didn't pay in full, but what he could give according to his age and position. Neither the driver nor the owner of the bus, or anyone else, could believe it. At the end, the owner of the bus came to me with tears in his eyes and said: "I have never seen anyone act like this, you have moved me and taught me like no one has ever done before." I hugged him while telling him that there are no offenses and that everything was fine.

Of course, I wasn't happy I had been hit, but the virtuous thing was to let go of my attachment to my new car and instead take the fairest action for everyone. If a small kid breaks an expensive vase you can't make him pay for it in full because the punishment is too harsh. The kid doesn't understand, so you make him pay a part so that he realizes the consequences of his actions. That's fair. This way I also planted a seed of virtue in everyone present.

The second attachment is the Emotional or Relationships attachment: it's the one that we have to any relationship that brings us affection or love, such as relationships of couples, with parents, children, friends, etc. Of all these, the biggest challenge is in the relationships of couples. Here again the biggest problem is believing that "your partner" belongs to you, that "your child" is yours. Then you start controlling them and the suffering comes from that pressure that, on many occasions, finally spoils and breaks the relationship up. Your partner doesn't belong to you and doesn't exist to satisfy your need for love, nor vice versa. A couple is a relationship of two free people who agree to share an experience together for as long as they both agree. No one belongs to you and no one exists only for you.

This is so taken to all levels, including the most difficult aspect such as sex. When you conquer this attachment, your partner can never again cheat on you, at most, what could happen is for your partner to sleep with another person, but you will no longer feel it as infidelity or betrayal, because your partner did nothing to you, nothing changes on you with that event.

This doesn't mean that we go having sex with whoever we want. Fidelity in couples saves a lot of suffering from STDs, unwanted children, jealousy. But if it happens, you should take the drama away and remember that your partner doesn't belong to you. Your partner did nothing to you. You should talk things over to see if there is love with the other person and your relationship is over, or if it was that the heat of the moment won and you can establish new agreements from forgiveness and conscience. Again, an example of how to conquer this attachment:

I had a relationship where I was getting married in a matter of months, then my partner broke up with me without giving me any reason and denying there was someone else involved. Two months later I found out that my partner was living with his new boyfriend who was certainly "cheating" on me with during our relationship. Six months later they break up and, in those days, walking down the street I run into the guy with whom my partner was cheating on me with. He stops and says: "I'm going through a hard time, I know I have no right to ask you, but I know you are a therapist, can you give me a hand?" And my answer was "of course I can" and I start giving him therapy and guidance so that he could solve his problems, without any kind of resentment or hard feelings, because neither this guy nor the person who was my partner, did anything to me. I chose forgiveness and compassion.

Here again, the most virtuous thing was to let go of my attachment to that relationship and help those who need me.

The third and final attachment is Mental or Identity: It's made up of your belief system and all the ways in which throughout your life, you have been defying and creating your identity or personality. If you previously considered that it was "your car", or "your partner", in this attachment you are convinced that you are "You". That you are "your last name", "your studies", "your nationality", "your economic level" etc. Because of these beliefs you have formed an image or identity of yourself and are now willing to do whatever is necessary to defend it. But this identity is not real. You are none of those things, they are just achievements and goals that you have accomplished, but not what you are.

If you studied medicine or accounting, you're not a doctor or an accountant, that's just your profession. But you were not born a doctor and you will not die a doctor. Your job and education are not what you are but what you do. You are not Spanish, Mexican or any nationality you were born with. Legally yes, but in terms of experience, 5,000 years ago your country didn't exist and maybe in another 20,000 years from now, it may no longer exist. God didn't create countries and nationalities, that is an invention exclusively of the human being to have a better functioning and to be able to live better in society, but your dog or cat don't take pride in their nationality, they don't care because they know it doesn't exist.

Believing that you are your identity is what causes you to be offended when someone else thinks differently or against your identity and ideas. You must remember that identity is just something you use because it is helpful, but it's not what you are.

Here is an example: A student breaks up with her boyfriend because he cheated on her, and after 8 months they both miss each other a lot because they love each other deeply and she would like to forgive him and return to him, but her family and friends tell her not to do it because "she must have dignity." My advice to her was that she had two options: keep her dignity high and suffer from being alone and not with the person she loves, or erase dignity from the equation and be with the person she loves by forgiving and reestablishing a firmer agreement with her boyfriend.

When you let go of your mental attachments and your identity, then no one can offend you anymore. If someone calls you an idiot, it doesn't make you an idiot just because they say so, as in the example of water, that doesn't turn into orange juice even if you yell at it, then if you are honest, you will accept that you have done and still do stupid things sometimes. So, when someone calls you an idiot the best reaction you can have is "certainly sometimes I do idiotic things, but I also do great and wonderful things too." If you want to become *one* with everything as we teach in Buddhism, it implies that you must be *one*, not only with the beautiful parts, but also with the ugly ones, that is, become one with idiocy!

Accept the three attachments as they generate joy and well-being for everyone. Learn to release and let go of them when they cause suffering. This is what "Conquer your attachments" means, you don't eliminate them but you learn to handle them yourself instead of them handling you.

It's like a waltz dance: "Hang on, detach, brace, detach ..."

This is a good exercise to identify and work on your attachments: Start with the physical one because it's the simplest. Take an item that has no great economic value and is not used or useful for your work, something that doesn't affect your economy (it can be a shirt that you loved and no longer fit, or a vase) and destroy it. It doesn't work to give it away or throw it away because part of you justifies that someone is going to use it now and you won't see your attachment. You have to cut it or break it so there is no denying the emotion. Then you will see the emotions that appear, that is your attachment and now you can feel it to dissolve it.

Severity in Virtue

I choose Virtue, and you?

Severity is doing your best and be decisive in something, in this case, in being virtuous.

Don't confuse being severe with being hard on yourself. The difference is that when you're hard on yourself, you treat yourself badly, hurt yourself and punish yourself, you are causing yourself suffering, so that is a vice. This is how you fall into the role of victim and enter an endless cycle of self-destruction. However, to be severe is to develop a level of supernatural willpower. It's the desire that, no matter what your mind or your emotions tell you or shout, you will have a strong will and strength enough to do what you have to do and remain in virtue promoting well-being to all, you included.

A virtue is a behavior that promotes the well-being of all and avoids suffering. A vice is the opposite, an action that causes pain and discomfort, a poison that pollutes and destroys. To remain in virtue, you must work on your ability to be aware and realize what causes suffering and what generates joy. Virtue is the new form of revolution. The word "revolutionize", doesn't come from the idea of war or confrontation, but from "re-evolve" which means "to evolve again." Virtue is the way you can revolutionize yourself causing well-being to everyone instead of pain.

When you discover that you have a problem to solve, instead of judging yourself for feeling bad or ignoring it, you must be severe and decide to resolve your conflicts and reactions as they appear, so you will be decreasing the duration of the discomfort and the problem. Being severe is taking responsibility for absolutely everything that happens in your life without ever blaming you for anything. In guilt there is drama, in responsibility there are solutions. Thus, you will be severe in the virtue of Prudence doing your best to feel good about yourself.

Therefore, before doing or saying something, you should ask yourself, is this going to hurt or benefit others? If the answer is to benefit everyone, including you, then don't hesitate, go for it, do it and everyone will be happy with your action.

But if the answer is to hurt, then why do it? The typical phrase "but everyone does it" isn't a justification for doing something inappropriate. Don't do it. You don't like being hurt neither. There are always ways to relate, communicate and achieve your goals without causing suffering to people, you must find these options if you want to be virtuous.

The great challenge and difficulty with virtues is that, in your environment most people don't understand the importance of this teaching. They don't yet understand the great benefit of choosing virtue, so apparently everything pushes you to resentment, revenge, hatred and confrontations. But you can make that difference and become a more virtuous being, bringing awareness and light to humanity. This means that the next time you see someone in a negative attitude, you should remember that that person is in the vice, is "poisoned" and you can opt to give them the medicine to heal instead of giving them more poison.

For example, it is to understand that for you to laugh, no one should suffer. Humor based on mockery, sarcasm and discrimination is common, but think about it, when you take part in such jokes someone is suffering from it. You wouldn't want to be the target of such mockery, right? Neither would anyone else. Be severe and don't agree to take part in this kind of humor even if "everyone does it." Instead, be creative and find ways to include those people in your entertainment and fun. Choose to laugh alongside others, not at others. This is a sample of how to remain in the severity of Equality and Compassion.

When someone is very angry and maybe even yelling at you, don't yell back, that is poisoning them more. Don't listen to the internal voices that want to believe in conflict and fight, but be severe and do your best to see they are suffering and remain at peace knowing that conflicts don't exist while apparently, they are happening. If you can do this, the person in front of you is going to have no choice but to give up and relax because they are not getting more poison to continue their war. You disarmed them and gave them the medicine they needed. It's difficult and it will cost you, but it's not impossible, hence the importance of severity.

If someone insults or criticizes you, you will perceive it as an offense, if you attack them back and return the insult, you just poisoned them even more and it will not have a good end. So, if they called you "dumb" they didn't make you dumb. Your essence is not altered by that insult, dumb is just a word, nothing more than that. It is your pride that is hurt. Let go of your pride and you will realize that nothing has changed in your life.

It is normal that in your life there are people who don't like you and don't agree with you, in your way of being or thinking. Don't pretend to like everyone because then you will live in function to others rather than according to you and your wishes. A lie told a thousand times is still a lie. Understand this and before that insult or offense, choose to forgive that person most quickly because now you know that they behave like that because of their dissatisfaction and pain. Don't hit back. Be severe, remain in forgiveness and again you will have given medicine to their illness.

All of this is not an excuse for the vicious behaviors of others, but rather an understanding of why they do it. It doesn't mean that you should always expose yourself to vicious behaviors or people either, this would be lacking the virtue of compassion for yourself. If someone hurts you, forgive them and as much as possible, try to make them see that this behavior is causing you pain and perhaps also to others. Give them the chance to notice and correct that attitude, but if you see that they are not interested in change and want to remain in that vice, you should still forgive and have compassion for them. Just take away from them, perhaps they will realize how or why they lose people around them and discover their own vice.

Another difficulty in being virtuous is wanting others to be virtuous as well. Obviously when everyone is virtuous, we will all live better, but understand that you can't wait for them to choose virtue for you to do so. Someone has to start setting an example and inspiring others. Decide to be that person.

Forgive those who don't know how to forgive.
Be compassionate to those who are not yet.
Remain in Peace in front of those who want to fight.
Treat equally those who want to discriminate and separate.
Be severe, choose virtue above all.

The evolution of the soul

Your evolution and ascension are inevitable.

Since you were born until today, you have lived countless experiences that have been teaching and helping you to mature and improve. To want to evolve is an innate quality of the human being, because thus we ensure survival and joy.

What are the steps of this evolution?

Different spiritual and religious traditions have defined this path of spiritual evolution in different ways, but they all have many points in common. Sakyamuni Buddha for example, described 10 steps or *bhumis* that we are traveling, while MahaVajra contemplates 22 steps called *VibhavaPad*. This difference is due to the fact that in the time of Sakyamuni, spiritual people were not considered until they had reached the first level of "Spiritual Seeker". Nor was it counted from Step 10 "Dharma Cloud", because at that point they were independent. MahaVajra however explains that everyone is evolving at different speed, therefore, all should be considered even if they don't have an active spirituality yet as such. In these 22 steps of *VibhavaPad* are contained the famous 10 *bhumis* of Buddha from step 4 to 14.

These steps of evolution will guide you to have a reference of where you are and what the challenges are in each case.

When a soul first incarnates in a human being, most of the time it comes from being some animal in the previous life and animals have no moral or ethical laws. Their sense of ownership boils down to "if you touch it, I'll kill you" and "if I want it, I'll take it without asking permission". This generates that souls, that just come from being animals, don't know how the human experience works and therefore behave like those animals that have always been, without respecting laws, morality, or ethics. They are souls without experience yet to understand what it is to live in society,

155

without the ability to understand what compassion is. This is the first step in evolution, we call it **The Animal**. Living in this way generates a very hard karma which causes that, after some lives, that soul agrees to follow the laws and society, not because it already understands it, but because it knows that not doing it hurts too much.

Now this soul spends some lives (quantity is not defined, as it depends on the soul) being what we call the **Grey Follower**, the second step. The quality of these people is that they follow the rules and laws as sheep of a herd without ever raising anything outside of them. This is a very good step because these people no longer generate the damage that the previous "animal" stage generates, such as robberies, physical assaults, rapes, murders and other crimes.

At this point that person has already resolved his physical integrity, that is to say their life is not in danger and usually begins to take care of their emotional and mental state. This causes them to get tired of being that "herd sheep" and want to understand and know more about life. It's not being a revolutionary and going against the system. Fighting is never a solution. It's the desire to want to understand oneself and to discover what is beyond materialism. It usually comes through the question of "what am I? what is the meaning of life?" and all these existential questions. Now this person has just entered the third step known as the **Spiritual Seeker**. It is usually characterized because the person is open to many forms of spirituality and usually absorbs wisdom through reading and courses with the deep desire to feel good, feel happy, be at peace and sometimes seek enlightenment. They are like a young university student who now studies not out of obligation but out of a desire for knowledge.

Through this search, they focus on themselves by ceasing to project on the outside and accept the suffering that is inside them by deciding to observe and solve it instead of denying it. It's not to create pain, but to resolve that which is already within you. It's the beginning of personal growth therapy. So, it's like sleeping, when you're dreaming and you have a nightmare where a stranger chase you while you're flying around the planet and you suddenly wake up and you realize that it was a dream, that it wasn't reality. Similarly, at this point you wake up to drama by realizing that drama is not real, but suffering is. The drama is all the extra, it's like "special effects" from your movie. Every time something bad happens to you, you suffer, but then you add the drama to make it more serious, sometimes to attract attention or just not to face it, and this only worsens the situation.

For example, if your partner leaves you, the suffering for the breakup is real, the fear of loneliness is real, but then you add the drama with phrases like "I'll spend Valentine's Day alone" or "my life is nothing without him/her" etc. This is drama, you have already lived without that person part of your life, which shows you that you can live without him or her. When you are able to identify and separate your drama from the real suffering, then you are in the fourth step known as **Spiritual Awakening or "Very Joyous"** by the joy you experience when you stop believing in drama.

If you no longer believe in drama and don't let yourself be convinced or moved by it, now you are no longer afraid to observe and face any suffering or pain in yourself. It can be hard, but there's no part of you that you don't want to see anymore. At this point, you usually want to observe and remain aware of all your suffering without exception. Until this step, people only do therapy when something hurts a lot, here you want to discover more and more without waiting for pain to manifest in everyday life, but look for it by digging inside to find both, the great emotions and the smallest and most subtle, for now you know the joy that comes from the liberation of each one of them. This fifth step is known as **The Stainless** because nothing stops you in your evolution. There's no drama anymore, so now nothing stops you.

Your mood is the sum of all the emotions inside you, when there are more emotions of sadness, anxiety, depression etc. then your mood is always negative or dense, however, if in the previous step you started to release all that pain and discomfort, you reach a point where you've resolved almost all of that pain or at least more than 50% of it. Then you experience a state of joy, love, almost permanent happiness 24 hours a day and every once in a while, something pushes you out of this state and it only takes you a few hours or a couple of days to get back to doing the work necessary to return to this state of blessing. It is the 6th step known as **The Luminous.**

All this suffering that people are resolving is mainly due to incompetence and ignorance of how to handle the three types of attachments. Therefore, to be enlightened, one must conquer (remember, not eliminate) material, emotional and mental attachments. When it happens, then you constantly experience, not just as a one-time experience, the true source of joy and love that is your soul. Now you know how to feel good and happy without anything outside intervening. You're starting to become self-sufficient.

There is a belief that enlightenment is only possible for some "chosen ones" or with special gifts, but this in part is a misunderstanding, and in part a form of control and authority by some teachers who don't know how to lead their students to enlightenment because of lack of competence, or because they are not enlightened. All the great Masters of history have said and affirmed that enlightenment is within everyone's reach and that it's inevitable that in one life or another you will achieve it, and I personally fully agree. Therefore, it's entirely possible for you to enlighten yourself in this life, you just have to do the necessary work to achieve it.

Others consider enlightenment to be the last step in evolution, however, Buddha spoke of 2 enlightenments: this first and a second enlightenment in which the person awakens to the Buddha state that will correspond to step 16. Another misconception is that enlightened people have supernatural abilities; It is not true, to develop supernatural abilities requires practice and training in those abilities you wish to develop and has nothing to do with people's level of consciousness. A person without so much consciousness but with so much determination can develop supernatural abilities, on the other hand, if an enlightened person has never been trained in them, will not have any. However, an enlightened person will develop them faster and deeper.

The sixth step, **The Luminous**, is almost the most important to achieve because it leads you to live a life of fullness and joy with yourself and your environment. And to encourage you, it doesn't require 10 or 20 years of practice, with a good teacher and following the proper meditation and personal growth techniques, many people have accomplished it in just 2 years. Imagine working hard (about 1 hour a day) on your emotions and meditations for 2 years in exchange for a life of joy and peace, it's worth it, right? Most likely your career took more years and more daily dedication. So, cheer up because you can do it!

These six steps are the most important, for it is where the majority of humanity finds themselves, and where the greatest liberation happens. We are going through the others in a summarized way.

Step 7: **The Radiant.** All that joy and blessing of enlightenment now radiates and spreads, without doing anything, to your surroundings friends and family. Now you sit next to someone depressed and without even talking, this person starts to feel better.

Step 8: **Difficult to cultivate.** After enlightenment, this step is where many spiritual people stagnate and sometimes fail to overcome for several lifetimes. It's because at this point, the level of blessing and wisdom is so high, that they are convinced to have "already finished" with evolution. There is so little and superficial suffering here that the ego convinces them to have finished everything already and to be self-realized Buddhas. For this same reason, it often happens that they no longer accept the guidance of a teacher, convinced that they already know everything. And it is precisely that arrogance that blocks them in their path. They're not finished yet, but rather are in a spiritual adolescence, so they fight against their former teachers.

Sometimes the soul remains in this state several lifetimes until it reaches a point where the soul asks: "Why do I keep coming back if I am self-realized?". Then enter into the humility of continuing to seek and advance on their spiritual path. It´s now possible for them to let go of their identity as a human being and as a soul.

Step 9: **Manifest**. In this step you will begin to manifest your desires with tremendous ease, sometimes you will just consider something to make it happen. It´s due to the great mastery of ego and consciousness achieved during the previous steps.

Step 10: **Gone afar**. Here you will experience absolute bewilderment. Until just before this step, you thought you had come far in your spirituality, but now you will realize the true distance. People may feel total neutrality towards all life experiences, there are no longer human illusions about achieving goals or objectives, but there is no depression or sadness about it, or denial of them. It is the beginning of the simplicity of accepting life as it is and is sometimes confused with reluctance for lack of experience and contrast with the previous drama.

Step 11: **The Immovable**. When your level of virtue is much more powerful than the traps of your ego and practically nothing can push you out of consciousness.

Step 12: **Good Intelligence**. Your mind and emotions have been so purified that you are a being of great intelligence and knowledge. Not only human intelligence but the ability to understand life and experiences.

Step 13: **Dharma cloud**. It corresponds to the Buddha *bhumi* 10. At this point you realize, not in your mind as thoughts, but as experience, that everything is dharma (wisdom). You walk, observe and live all experiences like wisdom and flowing dharma. It´s not yet the Buddha state, but you are on the way to becoming one.

Step 14: **The Virtuous or Arhat**. If all is wisdom, now you act as such and all your actions are virtuous toward all beings (not just people).

Step 15: **Irreversible Awakening**. Up to this point all previous evolution could be reversed if you don't remain active in your spirituality or practice, that is if you don't stay conscious. All the previous work has been to conquer the inner potentials and awaken them to virtue. But these potentials can fall asleep again if you fall again or choose unconsciousness. By reaching this step 15 it's no longer possible to reverse, there are already too many potentials awakened to consciousness; There are more potentials that drive you to be virtuous and to evolution than those that drive you to ignorance.

Step 16: **The Awakened or Buddha**. This step corresponds to the second enlightenment that Sakyamuni Buddha spoke of, which he achieved by sitting on the Bodhi tree. It happens when you conquer and awaken to consciousness 50 plus 1% of the potentials of your mind. The word "Buddha" means "awake" so it's a state, not a person's name. Sakyamuni was called that because he was awake, but there have been many other Buddhas and today there are still many in humanity.

Similar to what happens with enlightenment, some believe that the state of Buddhahood is not possible for everyone but for the "chosen ones" and this is again a mistake. Sakyamuni taught that absolutely everyone will attain the state of Buddhahood, for evolution is inevitable. Jesus said the same thing and MahaVajra thinks the same today. Think about it: if since you were born until today you have been evolving a little every day, what makes you think you couldn't go on and come to enlightenment first and then become a Buddha? Remember that there are no special or better beings than others. No one's going to save you. No Master or Guru can give you enlightenment because it's a personal work. As much as you love a child, you can't walk for him, the child has to take the steps himself. Just like you, you are the only one who can take your spiritual steps.

When you awake to being Buddha now you no longer die, but you experience ascension. Apparently, it may seem the same because your body will cease to have life, however, your soul instead of reincarnating may choose to remain ascended and create your own world or may decide to return and incarnate to help other beings achieve ascension. There are both cases, for example, Buddha remains ascended while the current Dalai Lama decided to return to help others. Non decision is better than the other, some decide to help as ascended beings and "pull" us up, others decide to help as embodied and physical teachers with whom we can interact.

When people reach this point, they are considered "self-realized" because their ascension is already guaranteed. The following steps of the *VibhavaPad* are achieved depending on the percentage of potentials that you awaken, above 51% in your mind, emotions, energy and body.

Step 17: **Trainer of people**. In some ancient traditions it is known as "men trainer" but this can cause the misunderstanding that it is not attainable or teachable to women which is not true, so it is more accurate to call it "Trainer of people", where both men and women are included. At this point, as the Buddha that you are now, everything you do serves to guide, help, and train people in their evolution. It's not that the trainer of people is thinking about teaching, it's that teaching is always happening. All your actions cause teachings, but you have neither importance nor control. Instead of considering "I am eating" you experience "the food is being eaten" without reference or importance to who is eating it. This way the trainer does not "teach", the teaching is happening.

Step 18: **The Care Taker**. The power and experience of Oneness is so present and obvious that you actually cease to exist and perceive yourself as an individual being. Creation is not millions of united components but a single reality which is cared for. Without reference to whom or what is cared for. God cares for all of the creation. You are God; therefore, everything is taken care of, you included.

Step 19: **The World Honored One**. Now you are made of so much light, you have so much divine presence that naturally people begin to pray to you because they experience that praying to you is the same as praying to God. The World honored one doesn't need prayers, in fact, does not even ask or demand them, nor does reject them, but accepts what happens with simplicity. This is what causes people to start praying to Buddha, Jesus, Krishna, etc. It is important to remember that you should not depend on anyone, not even your teacher. Fanaticism is not good because it eliminates people's freedom. Just like if you have a cavity you go to the dentist, but you don't worship him or her, when you have spiritual doubts or want divine inspiration you go to your teacher. Don´t allow yourself to fall into adoration or fanaticism. A good spiritual master will explain this to you, so that you know that gratitude and affection for them are good, but that you are always your own master.

Step 20: **Thus Come One or Tatagatha**. Being of absolute simplicity. Everything is simple therefore there is no simplicity anymore. It is embracing each event at 100%.

Step 21: **The Great Being or MahaSatva**. You become the embodiment of the universe and there is no longer an "I". You are not the great being, but Everything is.

Step 22: **Divine Incarnation or Avatar.** You are now a divine incarnation. It is when you manage to awaken not only in the mind but also in the emotions and in the body 50% plus 1 potential. Now that being is practically pure divinity. This is the case for example of Jesus, he conquered more than 50% of his potentials, which allowed him to ascend with his body included as a form of teaching, because his body was also awake as were his mind and his emotions. If you remember the 10 planes of existence, at this point you are awake to the truth 50% plus 1 potential of them all at once. When this happens now you know and live that all of nature is and always was awake. Everything is Avatar.

The level of consciousness at this point is so high, that it is often too much for nature and society to handle and both react against it. For example, if a cold day the sun is soft, your feeling is "oh, what a nice little sun". But now imagine having the sun right in front of you, blinding you completely and burning you constantly, then you would feel it is too much and you would want to hide from the sun and cover it up.

Something like this happens sometimes before these beings. They are too pure for nature and humanity. Fortunately, humanity is evolving and increasingly accepts these beings without much reaction.

These are the 22 steps or *VibhavaPad* in which all beings are and will go through. Most likely you've had recognized yourself in some of these steps, most likely where it sounded familiar is where you are at the moment. You are never in a single step or level, but experience at the same time one or two steps below and one or two steps above. To indicate your level, your level of consciousness has to be observed when nothing bad is happening to you, because when you meditate you increase your consciousness and when you suffer it decreases. That is why we look at it in moments of neutrality. Through your spiritual practice and personal growth, you get to experience the next steps wherever stage you are at.

Use this information not as a life mission or goals to achieve, but as a reference. Remember that evolution is not a mountain to climb and finish, but a path to travel, one more step every day. There are no goals, there are no objectives.

Unity

Observe people, plants, animals. You are that too. We are one.

Unity is one of the best-known Buddhist teachings and experiences. It's waking up and experiencing that you are *one* with Everything. The first time you feel this unity it's accompanied by an explosion of blessing, a very intense mixture of love-joy to which you gradually get used to and adapt, and finally it becomes a Truth that you live almost constantly.

From the point of view of the human being, we are not one. Each person has different and separate bodies, minds and emotions. We are independent beings. From the point of view of the soul something similar happens. Each soul, as you have already learned, is individual and independent, therefore, you have your own individual consciousness separate from other souls. The experience of Oneness happens on the divine level, specifically on 3th plane of the Holy Spirit or Interaction. It's when you access that plane that you wake up to the fact that you are one with Everything.

Why does it happen on the divine planes? Imagine for a moment, even if it isn't possible, that all people were women, that men did not exist. Then the words "female" and "male" wouldn't exist. We wouldn't talk about men and women because women would be all there is and it wouldn't be necessary to name them, it would be obvious because it would be the only thing. In our reality, we use the words man and woman to speak and refer to that apparent difference between the two.

If you translate this metaphor to God, the Creator, in the origin is totally alone, in plane 1 of existence that is the origin, there is nothing that is not God, therefore, there is no Unity because it is the only thing there is. Now remember that God or origin is not "something" or "someone" but is emptiness, the void just before creation happened, so here there can be no unity because in fact, there is only emptiness. From that void came All, it is the second plane of creation or the Son. Then we move from that, "there would only be emptiness", to "now there is only

Everything as the only thing", so again there can be no unity because there are no different things to join. If you look at your body in the mirror, you see a single volume, not a bunch of parts. It's from plane 3 that unity happens because at that moment, metaphorically, the holy spirit looks up and discovers the All and the Void, and at that moment realizes that Everything and Nothing are the same, therefore, Unity happens. That whole of creation is still God. Below plane 3, from 4 to 10, the separation is so great and the ego is so present, that there is no consciousness of Oneness. So, to perceive it, it's fundamental that you observe from that plane 3 of interaction.

This is what you feel when you live the Unity, at that moment you see apparently different people, trees, animals, houses, cars ... and you are aware that they are not many different and separate components, but that they are all a single experience in the which you are included. All of that forms one body instead of many components. You feel one with All and your heart lives an experience of Blessing before that love and joy of creation.

To help you live this profound experience of Unity, you need to contemplate everything that you separate in your life, and look for the origin of that separation you have set, in order to return to the point of union between both experiences. You must resolve your judgments towards both experiences so that through conscious observation, you'll find the point of union in each situation.

For example, there are no different skin colors, there are no white, black or yellow people, but all are one thing: Human beings. There are no homosexuals, heterosexuals, bisexuals or transgender people, but there are only human beings with the desire to live love and sexuality. Behind seemingly different religions, is always the passion for God. There are no different countries or nationalities there are only human beings living in different places. There is no spiritual life and a worldly or material life, there is only Life. There is no good and bad, but everything is experience.

Work on your egocentricity to stop looking exclusively at yourself and your life, so you can start to be aware of everything around you, the people in your environment. If you go by bus to work, you go with a lot of people around you and maybe are aware of it, but if for example, you go alone in your car, you completely ignore the rest without realizing that there are thousands of people with you, just one car away. But because you are locked in the bubble of your car, you miss the opportunity to live the experience of oneness while driving. How far does they have to be before you stop considering they are with you? Do you need to know them?

When driving, going by bus or subway, watch people and see that some of them are going to work so that you have internet on your phone, maybe someone else is going to serve you coffee, another is the one who builds the chair where you sit and so on. Each of these people are collaborating with others as infinite pieces of a puzzle for the welfare of all. Now include yourself too, you are one of those pieces and with your work whatever it is, you are helping everyone.

When you live in Unity you are never alone anymore, because you are always aware of the people who are at the next table in the restaurant or in the back hallway in the supermarket or in the building across from your house because everything is One and you are part of that One flowing.

Look at your body made up of millions and millions of cells, and feel that these cells are not individual, but together form your body as a single being. Let yourself feel that unity in your cells. Now also contemplate all people, both known and unknown, and feel that they are not millions of individual people, but together form a single being, that is the "Human Being". And go even further, contemplate all life forms and realize that they are not individuals, but form a single being that is the "sentient being" and these together with the planets, stars, solar systems, galaxies, etc. they form a single being that is the Creation. From the smallest atom in your body to the totality of the cosmos, everything is a single experience of a single thing: The Whole.

Train yourself to be aware of other people, even if it seems to be some physical distance or separation. Lead with the awareness that you and the people in front, behind and to the sides are like those cells of a single Being that exists in which you are included. As you walk down the street, drive, while eating with your colleagues or family, keep in mind this phrase: "Aware of everything and everyone." Do this exercise as long as you want, preferably daily and you will see the change in your overall perception.

All is One.

Illusion vs. Reality

As beautiful as a fantasy is, it's still unreal, choose the truth.

You have your way of being, thinking and acting. All this mark and defines your perception of life. And even if it is hard for you to accept, you're convinced that your ways are the best there is. The proof is that, if you knew a better way of doing things or expressing yourself, you would automatically switch to that better way, right? So that means that right now you think you are doing things in the best way you can.

This causes you *a priori* to always believe that you are right and your perception is good in every situation. However, note that throughout your life, you have changed your way of being and beliefs because you discovered some better ones. So, what makes you think that the current one is the real one and the definitive one? In fact, it's not. It's the one you have in this present moment until you discover a better one that will cause you more joy than the current one, then you will be convinced that this new one is the definitive one until you actually change it again.

All these beliefs form your perception and how you observe life. Therefore, your perception is like a filter or veil that stains reality according to that perception. If this filter is green, then you perceive life with a slight green touch. If your filter is negative or positive then you perceive life with pessimism or optimism. But in all cases, it's always tinged by all these belief systems.

How do we differentiate an illusion from the truth?

There are several ways, one of them is through the identification of the "symptoms" that manifest in your life. These symptoms are the facts that happen to you and are therefore undeniable. When something unpleasant happens to you, you automatically cover it with your veil of illusion and perception to make it more or less intense depending on your way of being and whether victimhood or pride is activated. That's not being objective. That's creating an illusion or fantasy in your mind and deciding to believe the fantasy instead of reality. You create these fantasies most of the time to evade your current life, other times because you very much want to live a certain experience. Having enthusiasm for something you want to do, is fine and you must work to achieve it. The problem is when you convince yourself that the illusion is reality, but it's not yet, it can be as beautiful as you want, but it is still not real. Then you live in a world of illusion that only contaminates and makes your mind and your emotions sick.

For example, you can be totally convinced that you don't have a problem with authority, but if your bosses treat you badly all the time or if you are fired frequently for problems with them, it's obvious you have a problem with authority. The illusion is to convince yourself that everything is fine, when the symptoms are that you always have problems with them. Another typical case is to justify in many ways, that you have no judgments about money, but if you have financial difficulties, it's obvious that you still have something unresolved on this issue.

You must decide to set aside the fantasy that is created by the ego and the mind and instead observe the symptoms, the facts that are happening objectively, to analyze them so you can find the right solutions.

The symptoms and facts of your life never lie, if you want a partner and you can't find one, that is not an illusion, it's a fact. The illusion is to justify that you are better alone than "in bad company" or that "all men / women are the same" when in reality you miss contact, affection and sexuality. When you lie to yourself with false illusions there's like a little voice that knows it's a lie, but you don't want to hear it because your fantasy is prettier. Truth and facts have a taste of reality that fantasy doesn't have.

This is what Buddha meant when he explained "Everything you perceive is an illusion", he never said "everything is an illusion happening in your mind". Buddha emphasized that the problem is your perception; it's your way of perceiving what is an illusion. It's obvious and undeniable that you are alive and that you exist, and there is no point in thinking that everything is happening in your mind and that we all agree that it is happening in the same way and at the same time. That's not true. You exist, you have a body that you can touch. Illusion is how you perceive and define reality.

An example for you to better understand is to contemplate your dreams while sleeping. In them a lot of people appear, some known and others unknown. In those dreams those people are representing different parts of you. If in your real life your sister is always supporting you, when in a dream you want to talk about support, then your sister will appear. The dream has nothing to do with your sister, but is a symbol in 95% of cases. Only 5% is about her.

When you wake up, the dream and the characters disappear because they are an illusion in your mind, just subconscious representations. Does this mean that dreams aren't real? No, they are real, but what happens in the dream is not. The fact that you dream is real, but the fact that someone is chasing you while you fly over the moon isn't true. The dream is real, what you dream is the illusion.

However, in your everyday life, every time you have a spiritual awakening, the world and people don't disappear, why? Because in our reality each human being and each living being are like a character in the great dream of Brahma (God).

All existence and the universe are happening in the mind of God, not in yours as an individual and separate being, that is the confusion of some people. The Creator is asleep dreaming and each of us is one of the characters of his dream. Therefore, just as if in your dream a character wakes up, you don't wake up, in real life Brahma doesn't wake up when one of the characters wakes up. It is necessary that most of the characters wake up for Brahma to do it.

We are a character happening in the mind and dream of Brahma and when most wake up, Brahma will wake up resulting in a "day" and later to a "night" creating a new dream.

Does it mean then that everything is an illusion and is false? No, just like your dreams are real but the facts that happen in your dream are not, your life and you are real. That is your error of perception, when someone offends you or insults you, when you feel betrayed, when it bothers you when someone lies, etc., that is the content of the dream, the illusion, not the reality.

Just as every character in your dreams is still you, in the great dream of Brahma (God) each character is Brahma too. Therefore, you are Brahma in the form of one of the characters and every person you interact with, is also Brahma. So, if we are all that God, how can there be conflicts and offenses? That's the illusion. Awaken from that illusion and you will be helping Brahma to wake up.

As we saw before, if everything in the world were made of stone, the stones wouldn't exist because it would be the only thing there is. If everything is illusion then illusion doesn't exist and everything is Truth.

Wake up.
Buddha

Love

You are self-contained love in your body.

Love in its universal and divine origin has no definition or objective. God doesn't love one person more than another. God doesn't love a child more than an adult or an elder person. God doesn't love a life form more than another. But all God experiences is undefined love for the whole creation, without separation or distinction.

This is how the world was created. From this divine origin, love began to come out and it gradually became densified. The more love became densified, the further away it was from the origin, therefore, the more separation and suffering it experienced. This continued until the moment when the perfect balance between love and suffering was reached. At that point the densification stopped because more of that would be too much suffering for the amount of love. It's in this place where nature and the tangible world appeared. It's where we exist.

You are the result of this densification of love that stopped just at that moment of balance, yet within you is still that original impulse of creation to want to receive more and more love and not want to give love back. Can you realize that you love being loved, but you find it hard to love out of fear? But what if you continue to receive and hoard love? The result is that you densify below the point of balance by falling into a life of greater suffering than love and joy, that is, sadness, depression, anxiety and loneliness.

Using a metaphor, imagine you have an empty 20-liter plastic bottle and you put it under a waterfall. As it fills with water, it weighs more and more, once it is filled, no more water can enter. Trying to get more water in, is just going to break and smash the bottle with pressure. Now for that water, if it doesn't come out and flow, it gets stuck and starts to rot.

One of the main causes of depression is this need to be loved and want to accumulate love without giving it back. Contemplate with honesty how many times you have demanded to be loved, even sometimes taking it by force. On how many occasions do you demand your parents, partner or children that they love you? And not only that they love you, but that they do it as you want, without even accepting how they can do it. Then you get disappointed and instead of observing your greed, you project it by blaming them and you end up feeling abandoned... just started your walk through your own hell. This is what causes so many people to claim that "love hurts" which is not true, what hurts is not love, but the excess of densification by greed to want more and want to control it.

If you discover that you are like that, you are not a bad person, that is how you have been created, but now you know that to continue demanding and even taking love by force is precisely what pushes you to your discomfort and pain. Make the decision to reverse the process now and instead of demanding love start giving it back.

Following the example of the water bottle, imagine now that we cut off the bottom leaving the container with an entrance and an exit hole, then you can put it eternally under an infinite waterfall and no matter how much water nor the water pressure, this container is able to take all the water and at the same time let it flow again. Thus, the bottle remains always full of clean and pure water. That's what you should do with yourself, cut out "your base", your greed for love, and let it flow naturally. Then you will discover that you always remain full of pure love.

Just as you want them to love you, so do all the people around you, so they all go around wanting to be loved, but not willing to become the giver and complaining at the same time about the lack of love they have in their lives. Be this person determined to reverse the process. Overcome your fear that it may end and you will be without love. Give it back, especially to anyone you took it by force. If you feel that in your life people take advantage of the love you give, it's most likely your karma for all the love you stole in the past. Instead of complaining, agree to pay your bill, to balance and start flowing from scratch.

If you want to have more friends or if you want to find a partner, the trick is to give love. There are millions of people who want to be loved, so love and naturally everyone will want to be with "the giver" as friends or couple and everyone will be happier.

This doesn't mean that you reject love when it comes to you. If you receive love you must accept it and at the same time continue to give it. In the beginning God was alone. God didn't received love from anyone and didn't suffer for it, on the contrary, God is that infinite source of love flowing. If you want to be like God, then give that love instead of keeping it as God does.

Remember a time when you gave love in a totally selfless way and someone felt deeply loved by you. Can you realize the joy you felt in loving them? That is your reward for giving love. When you love, what life gives you back is joy and satisfaction for being the cause of the experience of love.

The source of the pure Love of creation is the "undefined" love, it's not the "unconditional love" that we know, because it's in fact conditioned to the person who receives that love. For example, if you love your children unconditionally and another child hits them, will you feel unconditional love for that other child from another mother? Probably not. In addition, loving someone doesn't justify the incompetence or harm that this person's actions may cause or generate. Therefore, sometimes this unconditional love blinds you and makes you lose objectivity.

Above this unconditional love is undefined love. This is love free of all definition and purpose. When you say "I love chocolate" you are defining love for chocolate. When you say "I love my mother" again you are defining love for your mother or anyone else. This definite love is limited and it is what you try to accumulate. As always, you must find the middle ground between sometimes defining love to enjoy a certain experience, and cultivating undefined love at the same time to re-fill yourself with the original source and thus have more resources to continue sharing it.

To achieve this, during this exercise instead of contemplating "I love my life" or "I love my family" simply contemplate "love" without further definition, without allowing the mind to try to define or label it in any way. Breathe from your abdomen and gently contemplate the word "love" or *Prema* (love in Sanskrit) letting that indefinite and subtle feeling of love naturally begin to appear. Don´t force it to become big or become an explosion, give it time and it will grow gradually until it fills you completely.

To help you, visualize all your cells, bones and muscles formed by red, warm and tender hearts. It may seem absurd, but give yourself a chance to try. Without thinking of anything or anyone, but only the pure experience of unlimited Love. As if you were under that waterfall of infinite love without trying to keep it, but letting it flow, and every few seconds repeat in your mind *Prema*, Love.

Do it for 5 to 10 minutes daily and you will be reconnecting with the original source of pure love that you so much seek on the outside. Then you will be ready to give that love to others and flow.

Simplicity

My life is simple and I am happy.

This is the virtue that teaches you to embrace life, the present moment and any situation that is happening as it is, without judgment or interpretation. Life is simple and you complicate it.

Your habit of fighting against what is, makes life difficult for you. Watch how much you fight so that life becomes what you want. It's like wanting to change the trajectory of a moving ocean liner with your hand. How much easier would it be to flow to where the ship is going? How much trouble would you save if you were to flow where life takes you?

You have already learned that there are no life goals or missions to accomplish, so how dramatic can a change in direction of your course be?

Simplicity is not conformity. To be conformist is to remain always in inertia, without self-will. Simplicity is accepting to flow with the water of the river instead of going against the current. There will be times when, from within the water, you can alter the course and destination of the river, and there will be times when you can't do nothing but flow and enjoy the ride. The simpler you are, the simpler your life is and when everything is simple it is tremendously easy to alter and change the movement of the ocean liner because there is nothing that resists.

That's life, you are often in situations where there is nothing you can do and, instead of giving up and flowing, you keep fighting and complicating your existence. In a situation that you don't like, fighting against it actually reduces your chances of changing it. If there is any alternative to change it, be sure that it starts with accepting it as it is happening at the moment. You must get into what is happening, become one with it and from within, like a spy, if you can do something to improve it do it and if not, flow with that movement of life.

To be simple is to live in the *here and now*, realizing that at this very moment you need no more money, no more love, and absolutely nothing. It's a choice, but not a necessity. It's realizing that right now no one is attacking, insulting or offending you, so how bad is your life right now?

Right now, all you need is to be able to take the next breath, that's all. Can you breathe? Yes? So, at this very moment everything is fine. Don't listen to all the voices inside you that tell you it's not true. That is what causes complication in your life.

After realizing the simplicity of this present moment, now review your day. Of the hours that have passed, how many minutes have been bad? Maybe 15 minutes if you argued at work or with your partner, but the rest of the day could have been a quiet day if you had stayed in the simplicity of now and not in the drama of those 15 minutes in which you were stuck.

When something joyful happens to you, immediately you are able to accept it, embrace it and enjoy it, you don't doubt it for a moment. To be simple is doing the same with any experience you have. If you are suffering, don't run away from suffering and don't dramatize it. First accept it consciously so that you can come to embrace it too, as it's what you are living in that moment. If you try to evade it or run away from it, it will repeat itself and it will increasingly complicate your life.

Even if it sounds bad, if life is garbage, hug the garbage!

Another common mistake is to confuse simplicity with poverty or boredom, but this is a misunderstanding. There are arrogant poor people and simple billionaires. Simplicity is accepting that, if your economy allows you to, go to an expensive restaurant from time to time, go and enjoy it because that's why you work hard for. It's also accepting that, if you cannot afford it, then you can eat at a cheap restaurant or at home and enjoy it too. As you can see, simplicity is not in actions but in your attitude. If you can't agree to eat in a cheap place or drink cheap wine, you're complicated. If you can't accept an invitation to eat in an expensive place, you are complicated, because that is what life is offering you at that moment.

Maybe once in your life someone who loved you made you an expensive gift, a watch or a jewel, something you didn't expect and you had the typical reaction of "I can't accept it, it is too much". Is this being simple? If that person is giving you that valuable gift, it's because they want to and can afford it. The simplest thing you can do is take the gift and show your gratitude to that person. Never assume that you have to be given gifts, much less expensive; when they happen, accept them and when they don't, accept it anyway.

Don't confuse simplicity with false humility either. Suppose you cook a dish that looks exquisite and your friends say "What a good cook you are!" and you take the attitude of "no... it's no big deal, I'm not that good". This is false humility because in fact you know that you cook delicious, so by saying "I'm not that good" you are lying because you agree with them that the dish was delicious. The simplest thing you could answer to a compliment like that would be something like "yes, I also like how it turned out, thank you." Trying to conceal it, is to be complicated and to fake humility. Accepting the things that you are good at is being simple and humble, as well as accepting those you are not good at. It's embracing who you are and what you do as it is in every way. Just like before, don't expect people to compliment you about yourself and your qualities, that's being complicated. When someone says a compliment to you, accept it with simplicity and when no one does, accept it with simplicity.

To develop that simplicity, first look at yourself right now. With your virtues and your unresolved reactions and, instead of being harsh, embrace and accept yourself as you are right now. Stop struggling and fighting yourself. Breathe and with this awareness of who you are right now, contemplate: "I am simple." Allow yourself to fall into this simplicity of not fighting you. Just accept and embrace. "I am simple." Stay this way for a few minutes.

Then extend it to your environment, if you are simple then there is no other choice than your life to be simple, because your life is you. Contemplate now "my life is simple." And when the voices inside say otherwise, ignore them during the meditation, it's like a street vendor wanting to sell you something you don't need, just don't buy. Stay in "I am simple, my life is simple" state. And if your life is simple and all is well, then there can be nothing but joy.

Practice frequently "My life is simple, I am happy", or repeat the *Tathagata* mantra (simplicity in Sanskrit). Meditate on this phrase or mantra connecting with this feeling of simplicity and gentle happiness. *Tathagata* is the experience of accepting and embracing life, you, every experience and things as they are.

Do it daily for 5 to 10 minutes or whenever you feel like you or your life is getting complicated.

Embrace what is as it is. Embrace who you are as you are.

Be simple, be happy.

I am a divine act of God
I am white light
I am enlightened
I am Buddha
Wake up and remember!

Shivagam

Made in the USA
Coppell, TX
01 June 2021